MW00467325

In Search of the Human Face

This booklet contains transcripts, not reviewed by the speakers, of talks given at New York Encounter 2015

Crossroads Cultural Center

Human Adventure Books

Human Adventure Books

In Search of the Human Face
Proceedings of New York Encounter 2015
Crossroads Cultural Center

In Search of the Human Face

Index

"What is Man That You Are Mindful of Him?" (Psalm 8)
Maurizio (Riro) Maniscalco, Timothy Cardinal Dolan, and
Monsignor Lorenzo Albacete 9

Are More Rights the Right Answer?
Jennifer Nedelsky, John Witte, and Marta Cartabia 27

The Emergence of the Human Face
Kenneth Miller, Martin Nowak, and Maria Teresa Landi 51

Identity and the Challenge of Disability
Timothy Shriver, Sean Cardinal O' Malley, Jean Vanier, and
Barbara Gagliotti 79

How Can Education Bring Out Our Identity?
Darren Burris, Fr. Albert Holtz, OSB, and Fr. José Medina 103

"May You Never Be Content" — Msgr. Giussani's Legacy
Elizabeth Peralta, Kim Shankman, and John Waters 131

Searching for the Human Face...Online
Donna Freitas and Christian Smith 153

"What is Man That You Are Mindful of Him?" (Psalm 8)

Opening remarks by ***Timothy Cardinal Dolan****, Archbishop of New York, followed by a homage to the late* ***Msgr. Lorenzo Albacete****, theologian and a founder of New York Encounter.*

Introduction

"The supreme obstacle to our journey as men and women is the 'neglect' of the 'I'. The first point, then, of any human journey is the opposite of this neglect; concern for our own 'I', for our own person. It is an interest that might seem obvious but it is not obvious at all: a glance at our daily behavior is enough to show us that it is qualified by immense, wide gaps in our consciousness and loss of memory. Our first interest, then, is our subject. Our first interest is that the human subject be constituted and that I may understand what it is and be aware of it. Behind the increasingly fragile mask of the word 'I' there is great confusion today. Only the shell of the word has a certain consistency. But as soon as it is pronounced, the whole course of that sound, 'I', is entirely and only packed with forgetfulness of all that is most alive and worthy in us. The conception of the 'I' and our sense of it are tragically confused in our civilization."

Luigi Giussani, 1992

MAURIZIO (RIRO) MANISCALCO: Good evening, everybody, and welcome: this is the New York Encounter 2015, by God's grace and with a

Friday, January 16, 2015

lot of help from our friends.

I'm just a poor Wayfaring Stranger
wandering through this world of woe.
Yet there's no sickness, toil, nor danger,
in that bright land to which I go.
I'm going there to see my father,
I'm going there no more to roam.
I'm just going over Jordan,
I'm just going over home.

Kenny Lavender just played this song so beautifully. It's traditional music, but Kenny made it new, he made it his own. He made it New York—he made it New York somehow. He made it home. My hope and desire is that the Encounter be home to all of us. A strange home, though, because it will soon send us back into the world. We built this place; this was like an empty shell until this morning, believe it or not. We built this place because of the faith, hope, and charity that we have received. And we're here because we're still searching. We're building because we're still searching. We are today's poor wayfaring strangers, and along the way lots of friends, all searchers, will be with us during the weekend. The first one is a father, and we're extremely grateful and happy that he came to help us as we begin our journey. So, thank you, your eminence.

CARDINAL DOLAN: Praised be Jesus Christ. Seal it up, Jesu Cristo. He's right: you are at home here, and I'm the one who's happy and grateful to have the singular honor of welcoming you to New York City. That you would choose for this promising encounter this city, which I now cherish as my earthly home, means a lot to us here in New York. For the last seven or eight years [the New York Encounter] has been a source of real blessings for us in the archdiocese and in the wider community, and hear me say this: so is the radiant presence of Communion and Liberation here in the city. I see you in action here in New York. I meet you everywhere, and I can say with intense sincerity that you are truly salt to the earth and light to the world, and for that I praise God, and I thank all of you, and that makes my welcome all the warmer.

In Search of the Human Face. A cynic might ask, What is so religious about that? What's so spiritual about that theme? What does that have to do with faith? What's so Christian about that theme, *In Search of the Human Face*? "What is this?" a cynic might ask. Is this a meeting of dermatologists? Is this a cosmetology convention for makeup or something? *In Search of the Human Face*? We know better, we know better. We're not cynics. We know that *In Search of the Human Face* is actually part of the odyssey for the very face of God.

In the human face we see an icon of God's face. In the face of every human person, we see Veronica's veil, the image of Jesus himself. When God our Father looks at a human face, including our own, he sees the face of his Son. That vision is what inspired the great saints that we are so proud to claim here in New York. I guess, for instance, that's why a man named Saint Isaac Jogues would arrive here to love, embrace, and serve those considered to be savages and less than human, for he saw in their reddened faces the spark of the divine. Maybe that's why another of our saints, Kateri Tekawitha, saw her Lord in the hills, in the rivers, in the trees, in the sky, and in the winds. For her, the human, the earthly face of nature, revealed the very face and design of God. Perhaps that's why another one of ours, Elizabeth Ann Seaton, tells us she became a Catholic because the face of Christ she sensed in the Holy Eucharist so hypnotized her human gaze. I suppose that's why another New Yorker, Saint Marianne Cope, found the reflection of Jesus in the infected, swollen, pus-oozing faces of lepers as she worked with Saint Damien on Molokai. Or why Mother Frances Xavier Cabrini, on streets only blocks away from here, would sense the tears of Christ in the tearful faces of abandoned orphans of Italian immigrants. I'll bet that's what led Dorothy Day—another woman who walked streets very near here—to believe that such things as war, violence, hunger, racism, abortion, poverty, and homelessness contort the human face, and, therefore, defile the face of Jesus.

Is that why, for instance, Fulton J. Sheen [buried at Saint Patrick's Cathedral] throughout the radio and television stations of this city, told us that to be a Catholic means to find the face of the divine in the face of a mother and baby at Bethlehem, in the glow of bread and wine at Mass, in the face of an older woman working rosary beads through her arthritic hands in the back of church, and in the face and voice of an old man dressed in white who lives in Rome?

"What is man that you were so mindful of him?" asks the psalmist. You have made him little less than a god. The glory of God is man fully alive—something tells me it's this belief that animates the magnificent charism of Communion and Liberation each Good Friday morning when I have the honor and joy of joining thousands of you to do the Stations of the Cross over the Brooklyn Bridge.

I think how emblematic that is of the charism of Luigi Giussani, who wanted to build a bridge, yes: between God and man, yes; between the human face and the face of God, yes; between everything that is noble and enlightening and uplifting in culture and the Church, yes. For him, Church and culture were not oil and water, but more like vermouth and gin in a good martini. [*audience laughter*]

And that's why the face of God was so evident in the routinely somewhat disheveled face—with eyes ever-twinkling, and mouth ever-smiling—of Lorenzo Albacete, who in a moment we will recall with love, reverence, and gratitude. And that's why, in all of you, as I look at your human faces beginning this providential weekend, I also see a reflection of God's. That's why your theme is so pertinent, and that's why I'm very glad you're here and my welcome is so enthusiastic! God bless your weekend.

[Video Presentation]

LORENZO ALBACETE: Hi. I see that my notes are in a notebook that says, in Italian, "If you sin, then let it be original." [*audience laughter*] Sex, drugs, and rock 'n roll. Wow. Well, I'll start with a story myself. My own—not all the details, certainly—but just to begin to tell you why I'm involved with this.

I'm from Puerto Rico, so I grew up in a Latin American Hispanic Catholicism. Everything was penetrated by Catholicism. The culture was fully Catholic—in that sense, anyway. We had processions with the Blessed Sacrament on Corpus Christi, through streets in the old city that are known to be centers of prostitution, only to have the windows of those houses opened by the ladies, who threw flowers to the Blessed Sacrament as it passed by.

Just to go out; it was another understanding of morality. To me, the Church, the Catholic Church, was just like the air one breathes. It didn't have any particular piety. It was just like—I found anything else strange. But I went to study space science and flight physics at a university in the United States, Catholic University in Washington. It was the first time I came across a Catholicism that I had never experienced before. And it was, I felt, a defensive one. One that had underlined its identity, not in a proud, happy way, but in a defensive way. People, like, whisper to you, "She's a Catholic!" [*audience laughter*] and I found that very strange. But, what the heck, I wasn't going to stay there forever. My big desire was to get out and start working in scientific research, which I did.

And it was the first time I entered a culture in which there was no Catholic—in fact, rather, no Christian presence there as such. What was there was a bunch of people I loved and who were friendly; but above all I admired their passion for their work, their open-mindedness, their curiosity, the rigor with which they pursued their scientific investigations. I loved that they wanted to make it their own. I tried to learn from them and that was that.

However, they had a question. How could I be that way and be a Catholic? That is to say, they felt there was a split, an incompatibility, between my dedication to scientific research, which was not an average dedication—I had a passion for it. It is not 9:00 to 5:00 work. Sometimes you show up at 9:00 a.m. because you have to work, but you don't start to work until about 8:00 p.m. or something like that, because the rest of the time you're just talking with the other guys. It's when creativity strikes, that's when you do it. And it was just great! But they asked me about my religion, and I tried to answer that I saw nothing in my Catholic faith that was in conflict with science. But the more they insisted, the more I somehow began to—yes: for the first time my faith did not encompass all of my life.

It was, more or less, what Greg said. There were two things: there was my personal faith, and then there was my life. My life in the world, and my life—in this case—as a scientist, and there was everything else I was interested in. Not just in science—I was interested in everything, in politics, whatever. For that, I was all right. But when faith came, I somehow was expected to withdraw from all of that.

Well, I tried to understand that, and tried to understand how I could explain this split to the others, and let them know that this, in my opinion, this is a false split. That time coincided with the Second Vatican Council. I read about the Council in the *New York Times*, and they saw it that day, so they asked me, "What's going on in your Church?" My visit was presented as an entering into dialogue with the modern world. I liked that, and I thought, well, I mean, it's kind of the work I should be doing. Instead of me doing it I allowed the Council to do it, because I was engaged in the same thing, establishing a dialogue with these people. I loved finding out that the Church was involved with that, and I finally decided to take a look at that situation. I said, I will try to read the sources of the thought that was guiding the Council. That is when I began reading those thinkers that Greg mentioned: de Lubac, Balthasar, but also Paul Claudel, Bernanos, and T.S. Elliot. Because I knew they were sources that were quoted by people who were engaged in the Council and who I decided that I identified with.

I began my intellectual search for a way of healing this split between faith and real life. Many things happened. My being a priest is in a certain sense secondary to that. It was not part of that, I didn't think I had to be a priest to solve that problem; in fact, it seemed to be an obstacle because now I had a more official faith card to show. But then I recognized a vocation I couldn't resist, and followed it. Within my work as a priest I was sent back to school to get a doctorate in theology. It gave me a chance to systematically study the question. I would say to you that by the 1980s I had solved the problem mentally [*audience laughter*], and I am convinced that I have—that is to say—that I can give you a theological synthesis that in my opinion is perfectly satisfactory and unassailable and correct and everyone who is alive should adhere to it! [*audience laughter*] I knew the theoretical answer to it, but it was not enough. Nothing was happening. And so I stayed like that, waiting—I guess waiting for something to happen.

Then I met someone: a priest, who today is the Patriarch of Venice, the Cardinal Archbishop of Venice. Lovely, 'cause I now have an apartment in Venice. Anyway, it has its advantages. [*audience laughter*] We were both engaged in educational projects promoting that theological vision. But he was different. There was something about him I had never seen in a priest. He was the freest man I had ever seen. Yet he adhered to every teaching of the Church.

I'm a priest who adhered to every teaching of the Church, but I have to say to you that this adherence seemed to me to come at the cost of spontaneity, freedom, enjoyment of life. It seemed something that was closed and not open. And I also met other priests who were free and loving of life and open to anything: see, they didn't believe a damn thing that the Church taught. This man not only was both, but the one and the other were almost identical. That is to say, the reason he enjoyed life and was free was *because* of his faith in the proposal of the Church, his experience of life as a Catholic. The reason he adhered to the teaching of the Church was because these things moved him in that direction. They moved him in the direction of openness and embracing, of embracing everything that is good, interesting, and of doing this freely. It's just something you did not find, and perhaps difficult to find now. The two are not opposing each other but are working together as two aspects of the same thing.

So I asked him, "How come you are like that? How come you think like that?" And he said, "Well, you see I was educated by this Monsignor Luigi Giussani."

"Who's he?"

He gave me his name, told me his story, the Movement, etc., but remember that this was before and it was a strange thing to me. But fine. That was that. Every time he acted this way I asked him the same question and always the same damn Giussani kept coming up.

So on one visit to Rome I bought the books I found by Fr. Giussani. I read them, I loved them, I said, "Oh! He thinks like me and he has the same theological vision!" I remember going to a Cardinal I was working with and I repeated this, and he said, "Perhaps you should put it the other way around: you might think like Giussani." He said, "He comes first. This man is very important, he started this movement." And I said "Yeah, well, okay!" [*audience laughter*] Anyway, fine. So I now read Giussani and I saw that his theological answer was the answer I more or less already embraced. I didn't feel what Angelo Scola—this is the guy's name—it hadn't led me to the same kind of life and energy that it had in him. So I kept asking him the same question, and finally he got very upset and said, "God damn it, this is it!"—those are his exact words—"I'm not answering any more questions! The next time you come to Italy I will arrange it and you can meet Fr. Giussani and you can ask him yourself."

So it happened. I showed up in Milan, and so did Fr Giussani, only Scola wasn't there: he had framed us, he had set us up. He put the two of us together and he never intended to be there. So Giussani was thinking, What the heck is this guy here for? And I was thinking, What do I say to him? Hi, I like your books? Can you autograph this? [*audience laughter*]

It was a very awkward meeting at the beginning. It was lunch, and thank God for the lunch—there was great stuff to eat. I thought, This much I like of the Movement: they certainly eat well. [*audience laughter*] He said, "Tell me your story." I told him the story I just finished telling you, and at the end of this long conversation he asked me for help with the Movement in the United States. I agreed, and so when I got back to the United States I began to be more involved in certain activities of the Movement. Never did I think myself part of it until three, four, five years later. I was never recruited, I was never asked to join anything, my participation in the activities was purely because I loved them.

But I was noticing that, through them, through being with these people and living life with them, and doing these gestures with them, that the theological synthesis I had put together had become a life. Something concrete, a real life. An experience of life and not just a thought. Do you understand the difference? Because this is very important. The passage from an abstract discourse to an actual life. I noticed it happening in me. And finally I realized, without knowing it, I was now part of that family. I had found a home for my faith and my Catholicism, for my life, my vocation, and everything. So I announced it to them. There was no great cry of joy [*audience laughter*], we just continued doing what we were doing. But now I wasn't just helping from the outside, I was totally belonging from the inside.

That's my experience. Many years later I was to come across a line of Fr. Giussani somewhere, I don't remember the source. Because I decided never to know anymore, to free up part of my memory by not knowing any source of any quote or any Biblical verse, because it's all in Google. [*audience laughter*] I just put in the words, and somehow it miraculously appears.

Somewhere in there is a phrase where he says, basically, that you can have a right theology—for example, in this case, that Christ is the center of the universe. This is obviously the Holy Father's teaching, and you find these theological ramifications in Balthasar, in de Lubac and others, and you can hold to that, adhere to it, and it's true. But you must remember that prior to being all of that, prior to Christ being the center of the universe, He was a lump of blood in a woman's womb. And I said, you know, that's the difference. Christ as the center of history and of the universe is an abstraction, is a discourse, is an intellectual concept which is correct. It's correct. But so what? Christ as someone who began life as something concrete, as in the womb of a woman, that's different from the Christ that is the center of the universe. There's a fact there, there's a reality. This is where the problem was, in the split between fact and theory, or in this case, fact and discourse, fact and discourse.

Somehow or another they had separated. You had a discourse, which was essentially, on its own terms, correct, but which played no part in real life because it was not a fact of your life. You organize your life around certain other experiences. I saw that this was exactly what Fr. Giussani discovered and confirmed in that famous train ride of 1954, right before he was to make the decision that led to the Movement, in which he traveled with a bunch of high school students to a beach, on a train, and when he arrived there he realized that all of them saw themselves as Catholic, but the reality of Christ—Christ who was once a lump of blood—played no part in their lives. Christ the discourse did, as a remote figure, a teacher, an inspirer, whatever, but He was not a fact. On the other hand, there were other people, responding to other facts, that seemed to be generating a way of life. This is what the Church had done once. How did Christianity come to embrace the whole world when we got out of the Palestinian beginnings into Rome? It wasn't to just merely be a discourse; it was because it was a way of life. A way of life based on facts. If you read all those guys—those fathers, mothers, uncles, and teachers of the Church—they keep insisting on this. For example, when [Giussani] says, In our hands we have the books, where the theory is written—the Bible, and to that you can add the creeds, the encyclicals, the inspiring theological books. You know, in our hands we have the book, but before our eyes we have the event, what's happening.

This theory in purpose, or as the expression of an experience of a fact, of something that happens in life. And the something that happens generates within you, and therefore from you into the world, a new way of looking at reality. A new way of standing before what is real. And other than that, the culture, especially contemporary culture but really all culture, will interpret the discourse on its own terms, founded on its own experience, and it will make it harmless, non-provocative, boring. It will dissipate into the general mentality. It will have no freshness, no interest. If there's anything that can be said, anything when you read the gospels looking for this, anything that can be said about Christ, it's that certainly no one would have called Him a boring person. He was so provocative as to be offensive many times.

And yet, it was not just His words. Not at all. Above all it was His gestures. It was what He did and the way He spontaneously reacted. There was something that attracted people and repelled others, but there was something there. Their reaction many times is, "Where does this guy come from? How come he speaks this way? Don't we know his family? What kind of education did he have? Why does he speak like that?" Which led to the question, "Who is this man?"

It is this provocation that is the engine of Christianity. You take that away and reduce Christ to an intellectual proposal—then that's gone. I began to see that the problem we were facing is that we had lost that provocation. That, for whatever reason, Christ was not being presented by the Church as a fact that is provoking, surprising, but as something else: as a discourse, as a discourse.

Now look at the New Testament again from this perspective. You see this in almost every encounter. By the way, one of the great sources of my theology and worldview is Monty Python. [*audience laughter*] When you read the Gospel from a Monty Python perspective, it's much better than if you read it from any pious perspective. You see much more. There are some things that are really amazingly funny. Let me give you one example. The man born blind. Now, you might not think that's funny, but think of it this way. The guy asks for nothing. He's just sitting there, it's one more afternoon, you're born blind, and what the heck do you do? I mean, you just sit around, I guess; I can't imagine he's in great pain and now misses his sight, 'cause he never had it. He doesn't know what it means to see anything. So he's just kind of sitting around, and hoping not many neighborhood kids come by, because the kids could be cruel, you know, making fun of him and everything. But he hears noises and says, Oh my god, kids, but then somebody says, No, no, it's just some religious leader, his name is Jesus, and oh well, fine. He can't get up and follow the guy 'cause he don't know where he's at. [*audience laughter*] It's just something else that passes by, you see. Anyway, suddenly this guy stops. And there's this discussion with these people about whether it was his fault, or his parents' fault. You know this guy is saying, What the heck? Are they talking about me? But he doesn't know.

The guy's just sitting there, but then suddenly this religious leader stands and spits on the ground; whatever the discussion was about, his gesture, to prove his point, was to spit on the ground, make some mud, and throw it in the guy's face, who's just sitting there. Now, you think about what must be going through his mind: What the hell? This is worse than kids! [*audience laughter*] Or as Rodney Dangerfield, who has died, yesterday or something, said, "There's no respect!" So savage, they even throw mud at people who were born blind! And then so he probably says, "What the heck?" and Jesus says, "Go wash." "No, I hope to remain here with my muddy face." [*audience laughter*] So the guy goes, swearing and whatever, staggering. How the hell did he find the water? I don't know. Anyway, he washes, and Jesus on the other side goes on and the discussion seems to have ended, but one thing has happened: this guy can see. Does he understand why he can see? Does he know why this was done? Does he know anything about the guy who did this? Nothing, nothing. It really has changed, but it hasn't been due to anything other than the fact that, for one moment, he was in the same path as this guy. If he had decided that afternoon not to sit in that damn corner, but to go into another one, he would still be blind. I want to tell you, notice: the change began because of a concrete moment, in a concrete place, in a concrete way.

Now you know that he gets picked up by friends and foes, and immediately becomes a theological problem himself, because it was the Sabbath. The enemies of Jesus pick him up, they want to interrogate him. There begins that amazing masterpiece, page after page of the questioning of this lad by the authorities. Here he is asked, "Who was this guy? Why did he do this to you? Where does he come from?" And this guy keeps saying, "I don't know a damn thing!" Then he says, "You should know this thing, you're really the teacher." "We don't know where that guy comes from." "What?! You're the big authority and you don't know any of that?" Like, what kind of idiots are you? You should be here to tell me these things. Instead, you're asking me? Forget it. Well, not a nice attitude toward such authorities, but in any case, they bring in his parents and they say, "Of course, yeah, sure. Forget it. He's old enough. He can answer for himself." [They] sneak out. At the end they bring the guy again, and he says what I think is one of the most revealing lines in the entire New Testament. "Remember," he says, "I don't know the answer to any of your questions. I do know one thing: I was blind, and now I can see."

He hung on to a fact that was unassailable. All opinions are assailable, a fact is not. It's either there, or it's not there. And it generates a life, which as long as it is based on the fact, has a life. If not, it's just an intellectual discourse. Maybe it has a life up here [*gestures to head*] for a while, but it doesn't move you, it doesn't change anything in the way you experience reality and see the trees, and love your woman, and buy your food, or whatever. It's just an intellectual proposal.

This guy hung onto that fact and, eventually, was to see Jesus again. This time he recognized Him and believed in Him. That's one man. John and

Andrew leave John the Baptist and follow this guy, and when He says, "What do you want?" they don't ask, "What's true, what's false, what's good, what is it?"—they say, "Where do you hang out at? We want to be with you." Why? Because there was something, there was a provocation, something was happening to them. Just like the guys at Emmaus: "Our hearts were burning as this guy was explaining to us the Scriptures." It becomes an experience again. This is not sentimentality. This is a serious matter, but it originates in an experience.

Many years later, John or whoever wrote the fourth Gospel, sitting at the Patmos Holiday Inn, putting the stuff together, and when that day is recounted it says: "It was 4:00 p.m." Journaling theology did not exist, before a certain day, until 4:00 p.m. At 3:59, there was no journaling theology; at 4:01, it was all there. What happened at 4:00 p.m.? This guy ran into another one. An event that he would recount. Again and again and again.

Oh, one of my favorites is the paralytic coming down from a hole in the ceiling; that's as funny as it gets. The poor man thinking, This is the lowest moment of my life. [*audience laughter*] Then again, just think about this paralytic when he went home afterwards and could walk. I don't know what he did, I don't know, what does one do? I don't know, maybe he got drunk or something, or that night he went to sleep, the following morning he got up, and for a moment there was going to yell to whoever it is that got him up to go to the outhouse. And suddenly he went, "Wait, wait, wait a minute! I can go myself!" Then he opens the door and there are trees and the fields and the dogs. He saw them every day when he was a paralytic. But today he is seeing everything in a brand new way. So totalizing is the experience of the encounter with this Jesus, that even going to the bathroom changes.

Is that gone? Is it all over? This is a good question. Did that end after they killed Him? Oh, no, we now have the Risen Christ. Yeah, but...it's not the same. It's not the same. Is it the same? The Risen Christ for most is an abstraction. It's great He rose from the dead on the third day and that's wonderful—hey, congratulations! But this human encounter, within, if that doesn't exist today, then really it's all over. And no amount of orthodoxy, or morality, or philosophy can bring it back, if nothing happened. I came to understand that what Monsignor Giussani had realized is that the problem in making the Christian proposal is not just a theoretical one, but a fact of life, and creating a way of being together, which is not surprising since this is what the Church is, a way of being together, through which the discourse becomes a fact. And through that fact, we begin to see life in a new and intense, more attractive way.

In conclusion, I would just like to read to you Giussani's own words. In 1998 the Holy See, Holy Pontiff, called all the so-called movements in the world for a big shindig in Rome, and four founders of movements were asked to appear there before the Pope and 900,000 people—it was Pentecost—and explain what the heck their act was about. What had moved them, what distinguishes your movement, and what's going on. Well, if you're asked to give an account of your whole life, you either prepare or you take it as a joke. But if you decide to prepare, you gotta think exactly what it may have been. Fr. Giussani prepared, so it was interesting to see the first thing he said to the Pope, explaining everything. And he said, way before that day in 1954, that the question, the passion, the reality, the amazement that has moved him throughout his life, is the one provoked by the 8th Psalm: "What is man, that you should keep him in mind? Mortal man, that you care for him?"

It is a puzzlement, a curiosity, a passion about the human in all its limits. It's about the human identity: What does it mean to be a human being? That question, he says, is answered only by Christ, Who said, essentially, that one man, one's full human life, was worth everything in the universe. What would it profit a man if he gained the whole world but lost himself? This is what he tried to give to Christ, this passion for the human. Here was Giussani on Pentecost, standing before the Pope with 900,000 people there, and only one thing had moved him: the passion for the human. The same kind of passion the greats talk about when you read the great books and see the great works of art, enjoy the music, have your parties. That's why culture is one of our decisive areas of experience because it is born from this passion for the human.

It is this passion for the human, the encountering of this passion, taken to levels in the person of Christ that were unimaginable. He is lived today in the Church as a companionship so that He may be present to us with the same humanity He had then. That's what kept and generated the Movement of Communion and Liberation. Years later, the Pope sent a letter to Fr. Giussani, when certain important milestones in the history of the Movement had been reached. And he says to him, let's go back over the life and works of your Movement. "The first aspect that strikes me, Monsignor, is the commitment you put into listening, and to the needs of today's man." The Pope has taken seriously this passion for humanity. "Man never stops seeking," says the Pope, "both when he is marked by the drama of violence, loneliness, and insignificance, and when he lives in serenity and joy: he continues to seek. The only answer that would satisfy him and appease this search, comes from the encounter with the One who is at the source of his being and his action. The Movement, therefore, has chosen, and chooses to indicate, not *a* road, but *the* road, as a solution to the existential drama. A road you have affirmed so many times. The road that is Christ." The encounter with Christ. Christ experienced as a human encounter that provokes friendship, companionship, communion. This is the method: the Risen Christ is present. The Resurrection was for this purpose, to be able to create this way of coming together so that people of all ages, till the whole show ends, have the same experience as John and Andrew, and the man born blind, the Samaritan woman, and the paralytic. A complete change in the way of looking at life, because it is not just—remember—a physical change. Well, this physical change leads to more change, causes more change. It's a brand new way of seeing things. The paralytic can walk, but now he sees trees in a different way. Something has occurred that has hit him at the very origin of his look at life. This is what it is meant to be. This is what faith generates.

As the Pope said to Giussani, faith has shown to me an authentic adventure of cognition of the way you know reality. For it is not an abstract discourse—these are the words of the Pope—or a vague religious sentiment, he says, but a personal encounter with Christ, which bestows new meaning to life. The Pope is telling Giussani, I know this is what you realize, this is what you saw, and this is the purpose that sustains the Movement.

Finally, Giussani himself last year wrote a letter to the Pope to celebrate the 50th anniversary of the Movement, which we are celebrating this year. I find what he says here a rather happy way of expressing how, through the Movement, theory becomes life.

He says to the Pope: "Not only did I have no intention of founding anything, but I believe that the genius of the movement that I saw coming to birth lies in having felt the urgency to proclaim the need to return to the elementary aspects of Christianity. That is to say, the passion for the Christian fact, as such, in its original elements, and nothing more." His desire was to recapture, to understand, to relive, and to repropose that which happened to all of those people I mentioned to you. It happened then, but if it cannot happen now then the show is over. But if it happens now, then *how* does it happen? How does that format, that method—which is a big word for us—how is that method alive today? He says it was precisely for this "that I wove the unforeseen and unforeseeable possibility of encounter with personalities of the Jewish, Muslim, Buddhist, Protestant, and Orthodox worlds from the United States to Russia, in an impetus of embrace and appreciation for all that remains of truth, of beauty, of good, and of right in whoever lives a sense of belonging. Christianity is identified with a fact, Holy Father, as you yourself have stated. Not in an ideology. God has spoken to man, to mankind, not as a discourse discovered by philosophers and intellectuals, but as a fact. We are not saved by a formula, but by a person and the assurance which he gives us, 'I am with you.'

"In the great riverbed of the Church, and in fidelity to the magisterium [...] we have always wanted to do only one thing: bring people to discover, or see more, how Christ is present: the way, method, how to be certain that Christ is God, to have no doubt that what Jesus Christ said of Himself is true, finds his true answer in the attitude of the Apostles, because they were always asking, 'Who is He?,' struck in their experience by that exceptional nature of the Presence that had invested their human existence." Exceptionality, a marvel; you know something is exceptional, it's something that provokes amazement and wonder, and shows such a disproportion from the simplicity in which it appears that you are aware of the presence behind it. If that's not presence, c'mon, I have better things to do.

"Your Holiness wrote to us: before being a sum of doctrines or a rule for salvation, Christianity is the event of an encounter. Holy Father, for 50 years we have wagered everything on this evidence. It is exactly the experience of this encounter that lies at the root of the shaping amongst many of the Christian vocations, marriage, the priesthood, virginity, and the blossoming of lay personalities committed in life with a creativity that invests day to day life according to the three elements, two or three educated dimensions, always called from the very start: culture, charity, and mission.

"For this reason, we do not feel we are the bearers of a particular spirituality, nor do we feel the need to identify it. What dominates in us is gratitude for having discovered that the Church is life that encounters our life; it is not a discourse about life. The Church is humanity lived as the humanity of Christ. [*audience applause*]

WITTE
CARTABIA

ARE MORE RIGHTS THE RIGHT ANSWER?

*A discussion with **Jennifer Nedelsky**, Professor of Law, University of Toronto, and **John Witte**, Professor of Law, Emory University, moderated by **Marta Cartabia**, Vice-President of the Constitutional Court of Italy, on the relationship between the search for identity and the proliferation of new individual rights brought about by social changes*

Introduction

It is a common experience of contemporary life that more and more political and social issues are framed in the language of "rights." Whereas our culture is usually very uncomfortable with any kind of appeal to universal moral truths or to a "natural law," it is quite willing to recognize all sorts of "human rights," both of individuals and of social groups. Hence, the "proliferation of rights" is not at all an academic question, but a social trend that we all can encounter in our daily circumstances, at our workplace, or at school. This discussion is an attempt to ask some fundamental questions, such as: why are there rights in the first place? What determines what they are and who enjoys them? Can this process be abused? What role should rights play in our legal system?

MARTA CARTABIA: Good morning, everybody, and welcome to this first panel on human rights. I'm really honored to share the podium with two distinguished people, Professor Nedelsky and Professor Witte. First of all let me introduce myself, because I assume that I'm not known either. I'm also not sure in what capacity I was invited to be here—professor of law, constitutional law, European law, member of the Constitutional Court,

Saturday, January 17, 2015

or, most likely, as simply a friend of many of the people here and the New York Encounter.

Our topic today is about human rights, something that was already in the scholarship and reflections of Professor Nedelsky and Professor Witte. Professor Nedelsky teaches at the University of Toronto, and previously at Princeton. Her scholarship has concentrated on family theory, legal theory, American constitutional history, and interpretation. Her most recent book, *Laws Relations*, was awarded an important prize, the McPherson Prize. It was in reading that book that we became very interested in understanding her interpretation of human rights and the human face of the person that bears this right. She has a number of academic positions, but I want to stress here that she's also the mother of Tucson, Michael, and Daniel.

Professor Witte is a world-renowned scholar on legal history, and his scholarship is within marriage law and religious law. He's the Director of the Center for the Study of Law and Religion at Emory University, and he edits a number of book series, among which is *Law and Christianity,* covering law and religion, marriage, and family. He also has two daughters and three grandchildren.

So let's introduce our topic on human rights, individual rights, or constitutional rights. This instrument of the legal order has a glorious history. It's difficult to really decide the origin of them, but for sure after World War II they flourished as a reaction to the wrongs of the totalitarian regimes in Europe and elsewhere. Let's just recall the Universal Declaration of Human Rights in 1948: it has greatly contributed to protecting individuals, the weakest persons, against all forms of oppression and despotic exercise of power. Over the last twenty years, however, in Western countries, rights talk has become more insistent, to the point of almost being overused. Every personal or social need and desire is claimed as a right.

In a way we can say, using the words of Noberto Bobbio, a prominent Italian political philosopher, that we are in an age of rights, an age of new rights. We often speak, for example, of a right to a clean environment, a right to health, a right to marry, a right to a house, a right to live, a right to die, a right to have a child, and so on. Rights have become the common currency of every public discourse.

So my first question to both our speakers would be: Why are rights so successful? What is their added value? Why do we need, in the end, more rights, or do we? Professor Nedelsky.

JENNIFER NEDELSKY: Thank you, it's a great pleasure to be here. When we think about why we would need more rights, I want to start with a question: What is it that rights do for us? Calling something a right highlights what values are of primary importance. What values stand out for special consideration? That's the first thing they do. Legal rights, especially constitutional rights, provide a means for holding democratic decision-makers, like legislatures, accountable to those core values. Rights are a way of saying that when core values are threatened by government action, the decision-makers can be required to justify those threats. To explain why maybe they don't really harm the core values, or why they might be justified in any case, as in the Canadian Constitution, where it uses the phrase: justifiable in a free and democratic society. If justifiable, it can be okay to interfere with rights in some cases. But to call something a right, a legal right, a constitutional right, is to say that it's not enough just to support a policy by saying it's what the majority wants; and that's a very important contribution to the idea of rights. So, then, the question of new rights and why we need them is a question of new values or a new recognition of their importance. For example, when people come to see their relationship to the earth as not simply an instrumental one where the earth is something from which individual property owners can extract whatever they want, whenever they want, but instead is a relationship of responsibility and care that is consistent with a respectful relation to creation.

Then people may start to talk about a right to a clean environment as a way to express the priority they want governments to attach to the care of the earth. It's a way of holding governments accountable to that value by saying that majority rule is not enough. Or, perhaps, also I demand to rethink what we mean by property rights. Now, I will say that it's an open question in my mind whether the language of individual rights is the best way to express such a relationship of care and responsibility toward the earth, but the problem is that rights is the almost universal language to attach a priority to value. So, that's the language people reach for when they want to bring attention to a value that has not received enough protection. The language of a right to a clean environment can lead to rethinking of other rights such as property rights, and bring in a greater degree of responsibility into the meaning of those rights when rights are understood in relational terms.

Even individualistic-sounding rights can bring an attention to interdependence to the core values we really care about; and finally, because rights language is used all over the world, I think it's more helpful to try to think about the best way to understand rights, the best framework and language used to analyze the debates about rights, rather than to try to reject the use of the term.

CARTABIA: Thank you, Professor Nedelsky. So, rights bring more attention to the values that we consider important in our social lives, even when the majority does not pay attention to them. Majority rule is not enough. What would you like to add, John?

JOHN WITTE: Well, first of all, I want to add a warm word of thanks to professor, judge, and martyr Cartabia, and for the organizers of the Encounter series for having us here.

I want to thank Professor Nedelsky for stealing my thunder because I was going to say much of what she just said, and so I'm going to play to my proclivities as an historian to suggest to you that this business of trying to articulate aspirational rights is a normal part of the rights tradition, and indeed has been in the West for nearly two millennia. The question of the aspirational right that is set forth is like a spring tide that comes through and seeks to break new ground, and inevitably that tide recedes in the question of the resilience of those rights, and turns on some of the questions that Professor Nedelsky raised to the table. So, I could take you on a quick historical tour because we've been doing rights in the West for an awful long time. Back in classical Roman law we had plain, uncontroversial rights: the property inheritance, marriage and commercial relationships.

We also had aspirational rights, especially the rights that Christians were pressing for: freedom of conscience and the right to free exercise of their faith as minorities who were persecuted and beleaguered, and those rights became actualized in the Edict of Milan of 313.

In the medieval canon of the High Middle Ages, we have the Catholic Church start with a powerful aspirational right, the freedom of the Church—*libertas ecclesiae*—to break it free from secular control and authorities. Then it ultimately received its freedom, having the opportunity to implement a complex medieval canon law that had a whole latticework of public and private and penal and procedural rights for all of Christendom. Along the way, secular institutions did the same thing. Remember, this is the 800th anniversary of the Magna Carta, which put into common law the first rights of due process, the first rights about property, the first rights of taxation. In the 16th century, the Reformation broke out in the name of Christian freedom, an aspirational norm which Protestants in that day sought to put into place to overcome what they perceived as the tyranny of Church and state. They tried to put into place a secular rights apparatus with countervailing conversations made by the Salamanca jurists in Spain, who developed a very rich understanding of rights for the Church and for the state, and set forth aspirational rights such as rights for the Indians.

It is a telling anecdote that, in 1650, every one of the rights that would appear a hundred and fifty years later in the U.S. Bill of Rights and the French Declaration of the Rights of Man—had already been defined, defended, and died for by Catholic and Protestant Christians. As professor, judge, and martyr Cartabia said, in 1948 the devastation visited on all of humanity by World War II gave impetus to set forth an aspirational declaration of rights.

We have been doing this business of trying to define new rights as part of the Western legal tradition from the start. I think the question becomes, How do those rights become implemented? What makes them resilient? How they ultimately soak into the polity in a responsible way? I suggest three quick things. One, those rights claims ultimately have to be solidly grounded. They cannot just be a whimsical subjective wish list. They have to be grounded in some aspect of fundamental human nature, in moral duty, in the common good, or something else that gives it resilience over time. Secondly, the right has to be practically feasible over time in the legal culture and social condition in which it has been implemented. It could be a high-flying right—like due process of law or equal protection under the law—that takes a long time, but it has to be something practical, it has to be something that the institutional and social and cultural condition can accommodate over time. And third, it has to be properly directed not just as a wish list that the state can fulfill, like a Christmas list, but it has to be a right that ultimately is woven into the community and draws upon multiple institutions to be implemented and made real.

The relational theory of rights that Professor Nedelsky's going to talk about, I think, will come out in this; in our subsidiary theories of the Catholic tradition, or sphere sovereignty theories of the Protestant traditions, we have a recognition that a variety of institutions alongside the state are in the business of vindicating the rights claim that's made. The right of a child, say, begins in the family, begins with his or her parents, begins in the communities of which they are a part, long before the state gets involved.

Resilience turns in part on multi-institutionality. And so I wouldn't be despairing of new rights talk, I would simply say that, over time, rights talk is going to have to prove its resilience through some of these factors.

CARTABIA: Thank you very much, John. Thank you for this overview of the long history of human rights that starts long before World War II. This long history proves in itself the importance of human rights. No doubt that today one of the more relevant benefits of the rights, of course, is that they put the individual at the center. Thanks to human rights, the person becomes a subject as opposed to an object of public choices. She becomes a protagonist of public life, and this is every day in the new wave of European Constitutions born out of World War II, where the person, a human being, is the center and the core around which all the institutional structure is built up.

But my next question—it is very related to the general title of this New York Encounter—would be what kind of person is implied in the rights talk? Who is the rights bearer? What are his and her personal traits? And

I would like to add a word related to the new rights discourse, because the new rights often come from a process of fragmentation. Especially those that are a result of the principle of non-discrimination tend to capture a single feature of the human person and to insist only on that feature. Principles of non-discrimination in Europe, for example, generated the rights of women, the rights of the LGBT person, the rights of Roma, the rights of migrant people, the immigrant workers and the indigenous people, the disabled people, and so on and so forth. The result is a sort of scattering of the human person on the basis of a single, or a relevant, feature of her identity.

Considering this trend of new rights, what is the human face of rights, and what should be the human face, the human face of the rights that are there? Maybe John wants to start first. Difficult question, right?

WITTE: How many hours do we have? Well, I'd say the face of human rights is every person, every person who's a creature of God and every person, as the Vatican fathers say, who has rights flowing from his or her very being. And so the human rights bearer, the human rights claimant, is not only the rational, calculating adult that we learned about in political liberalism 101, but is also the mentally disabled and the persons who have lost their capacity to reason. It is the sick and the dying and the comatose who have lost their capacity to calculate. The human face of human rights is not only the adult, but also the child, the babe in arms, and in my view, also the baby in the womb who's viable. It's not only the man but also the woman. It's not only the native but also the immigrant. It's not only a neighbor but also a stranger. Not only the friend but also the enemy. Not only the citizen but also the criminal. Every person, *qua* person, is a rights bearer, and has rights flowing from her or his very nature.

I think that's fundamentally what our rights framework has to start with, and that's what's rooted in the concept of human dignity that the declaration articulates. But I think it's also important for us to realize that in the twentieth and twenty-first centuries, what's equally critical are the rights of the group, and the rights of groups, the rights of the Church, the rights of the family, the rights of the corporation, the rights of the union, the rights of the school, the rights of a number of different voluntary associations—are an equally important part of our rights discourse, particularly since it has become so pervasive. We have various ways of thinking about the group as a rights holder.

Classically, it was an extension of the Church or an extension of the king. Now, we view the person as a fictitious person when he or she comes as a corporation, or as a group. But then the idea is that a group has legal personality, and that this legal personality is respected. The rights for this group to operate as a group are critically important parts of the protection that is accorded to the community that respects human rights. And thus are a particularly important issue for people of faith who find in the world today that basic corporate rights of a religious group, including the Christian Church, to exist is not something that one can assume automatically.

We have 198 independent nation states or territories around the world, and in more than 75 of them legal personality for religious groups, including churches, is deeply contested, and the ability of that church to exist as a whole property, to maintain standards of entrance or exit, to publish literature to worship, to be able to engage in relationships with their fellow believers at home and abroad are deeply contested. So part of the human face of human rights is the collection of people that gather in bodies, which bodies themselves take on a corporate identity, which needs to be respected equally well in a human rights world.

CARTABIA: Thank you, John.

NEDELSKY: Thank you. I'm going to try to pick up on one of the issues of the practicality of rights and what makes them real for people's real lives. I think of as tools what are sometimes called "special rights" of the disabled and the elderly. The rights of the disabled, of the elderly, of women, bring attention to the embodied reality of the rights holder. The person with rights always exists in a particular body, in a particular context. We cannot know how to make rights real in a practical way, without paying attention to these dimensions of human reality. Of course, we can and should invoke big abstractions like equality and dignity, but we can only know how to make those abstractions real by paying attention to the concrete particulars of the people whose rights we are concerned with. I think some framework of rights like those that take social, economic, and cultural rights seriously are better suited to paying attention to these concrete particulars.

When one is used to asking whether a given right—like, say, the ability to participate equally and effectively in the democratic process—is itself dependent on a certain level of economic equality, then one develops the capacity to pay attention to context and the particulars of human needs and abilities in trying to figure out how to give rights practical meaning for all. Some structures of rights are more likely to give a fully human face to rights. Even as we also ask ourselves whether these rights must be understood not simply in human terms, but in relation to the wider creation with which we share the earth.

Special rights, like the rights of the disabled, can be misused, to make disabilities, say, the single feature of the person, the center of a person's identity. That's a downside of this focus on special rights. They can also be understood in ways that highlight the vulnerability and interdependence of all people, and to structure our mutual responsibility accordingly. I think the United Nations Convention on the Rights of Persons with Disabilities is a good example of this approach to particular rights. So, while there can be bad consequences of a proliferation of special rights, if we approach them from a relational perspective, such rights can turn our attention to the necessary specificity and context that can make rights real for everyone.

CARTABIA: Thank you, thanks to both of you for recalling us to the complexity of human experience. Rights being not just for an individual, but also for a group. Let me start with a quotation that's a little bit provocative and can be thought-provoking.

Speaking about the European Union, Joseph Weiler says that the insistence on rights, at least in Europe—I don't know about the American continent—but probably it's the same—has put "the individual in the center, but the result is a society of self-centered individuals, so that the result of the insistence on rights is an excess of individualism, narcissism, selfishness; and these are costs that our society is paying for this insistence on rights."

Are More Rights the Right Answer?

Rights turn human desire and needs into claims, and each claimant has a defendant in front of him. My next question to you would be: Do you think that rights inevitably produce or encourage a conflictual society, or to encourage people to break relationships? Do they shape relationships as litigations?

NEDELSKY: As I see it, what rights actually do is shape relationships. Now those relationships can be conflictual ones. They can be highly individualistic. Depending on how rights are understood and implemented legally, they can turn our attention to reciprocal obligation and the realities of human interdependence; or, they can highlight individual entitlement as if it had no consequences for relationships with others.

It's not rights as such that determine what sort of relationships people have or what sort of values are fostered; it's how we define particular rights, and whether we develop a relational habit of thought when we engage in debates about rights. When people see that rights always structure relationships, say, of power, of trust, of responsibility or lack of responsibility, then the question is how one wants rights to structure relationships in order to foster what values.

For example, the relationships fostered by no-fault divorce: Should we see them as providing vital freedom of choice without destructive patterns of blame, or are those relationships also free of norms of commitment and responsibility? Is there a way for the right created by family law to foster both freedom and responsibility? Or in a different context, does a factory owner have responsibility to her employees when she's thinking about closing the factory? Should our rights of property include such responsibility, or should we say that the relationships created over 20 years of production play no role in the individual rights of the factory owner?

The question is not whether there should be property rights; the question is how we should define those property rights and what kind of relationships will follow from that definition. What values—say, quality, responsibility, attention to community, freedom, entrepreneurship, financial gain? Some of these values will be in tension with one another. What values will be fostered by the structure of relationships that a given definition of property rights creates? Those are the kinds of questions that will make a difference in the impact that rights actually have.

CARTABIA: John?

WITTE: I'm not a sociologist or anthropologist, but certainly there's plenty of anecdotal evidence, in my view, of a culture of growing narcissism and self-indulgence and selfishness. There's certainly well-documented increases in litigation. And, as we've heard, there is certainly an explosion of rights claim that have beset the culture over the last twenty or twenty-five years. The question is whether those three things are related. Whether this new excessive individualism is a consequence of rights, and whether litigation is necessarily a good or a bad thing. And one of the things that I would like to suggest is that it's not necessarily true that a robust regime of human rights leads automatically to individualism and selfishness and the narcissism that we see. After all, historically, both Catholic and Protestant communities in the West were rights cultures in part. And it's not necessarily a bad thing in seasons of cultures to have major campaigns of litigation to get things done.

I think the issue is how a culture and community find ways of resolving disputes, of avenging wrongs, of building relationships, of crediting the reasonable expectation and reliance interests of members of society. I think what's emerged in the late twentieth and twenty-first centuries is the fact that, increasingly, rights have become the discourse for thinking about how to achieve those forms of dispute resolution. And, increasingly, without any other universal authority that's respected and recognized, we turn increasingly and reflexively to the state to get our interests vindicated. We do that through litigation and lobbying, and with a massive, massive bar of public interest litigation afoot the litigation simply escalates as we go forward in time. But I dare say that there are also hopeful signs of change, which in my view are salutary.

Mediation, arbitration, alternative dispute resolutions of various types, defendant-victim reconciliation programs, restorative justice programs—these are beginning to become increasingly common in different pockets of the West, including the United States, and have begun to blunt some of these excesses of narcissism and self-interested litigation. Religious communities, schools, neighborhoods, and other institutions of civil society are taking stronger roles at the front end of education, creating prudential norms of interaction with their neighbors. But they're also at the back end, providing informal, but none-the-less effective vehicles of exchange, of resolution of disputes that are before them. Particularly religious communities, and among them notably the Catholic Church, have a massive internal religious legal system that is becoming increasingly resilient in its ability not only to deal with high-level official things—clerical things, for instance—but also in providing a living legal system for the voluntary faithful to turn to in lieu of turning to courts. In my view that's a healthy development simply from a public policy standpoint; it's also a healthy development from a Christian perspective that I happened to come with, because when we turn to our Bible we regularly see admonitions in the New Testament about working out disagreements with your brother or your sister: go to your brother and sister and seek to work it out. If that doesn't work, bring a friend or two or a member from your community with you, and if that doesn't work out, go tell it to the Church, we are told. And one of the things that New Testament teaching underscores for us is that we do not have to turn to the state to do all of the hard work of vindicating our interests.

When building new relationships with our neighbors and exercising the love command that we have, we're sometimes required to turn the other cheek. I have an interesting quote from the great U.S. Supreme Court Justice Oliver Wendell Holmes, Jr., who said more than a hundred years ago: "It's a very sad society indeed that looks to the courts to make all of its hard decisions for it." And I think that admonition from a hundred years ago, when there wasn't narcissism, there wasn't litigation, there wasn't a human rights explosion at the level we have today, is one that echoes loudly for us and I think it encourages us to find alternative ways of living with, and loving, our neighbors as ourselves.

CARTABIA: Let me stress once again a point that I understand is a common point of view to our speakers: rights, per se, are not a bad or a good thing; they are shaped according to the cultural background of each society. We can have individualistic rights that encourage litigation and contractual relationship, or we can have rights that promote a different culture, provided this culture has already some roots in this society.

There is an interaction between the legal tools and the cultural background of each society that can make a different, completely different, result with the same legal tools of individualistic rights. Let's turn to a specific question for Jennifer Nedelsky that is rooted in her last book, *Laws Relations*. In this book, you call for a relational understanding of human rights, which is a strong correction of the general discourse on human rights that is practiced in our societies. You start from a rich account of the human person, one that cannot be reduced to the roles of, how do you say that? It is described by John Rawls: a rational agent able to make his own choices. Rationality and free choices, then, are the most important ingredients of a certain kind of rights discourse.

On the contrary, you stress that the person who is embodiment is relational, is affected, and is rational as well. In Europe there is an interesting debate aimed at a Catholic scholarship that contrasts the individual considered as an abstract person, and the person who is taken with all his richness, with his comprehensive experience of the self which includes rationality as well as affection, singularity as well as relationality.

It is very close to the multi-dimensional self that you describe in your wonderful book. Do you think that this rich understanding of the human person can fit into the right practice as we know it today in our age, or is there something that is inescapable within? And if yes, what are the major points that we need to correct in our practice on rights?

NEDELSKY: Thank you. I want to have two parts to this answer. First, to say a little bit more about what it means to think about rights in relational terms, and then, secondly, to ask why are they still rights when we're thinking about them relationally instead of individualistically? What is it that makes sure they don't lose their function as rights? So the first thing is to repeat what I said before, that all rights structure relationships. Now what's important here is I'm not arguing that that's what rights should do; I see this as just a fact about legal rights. That's what they do, they structure relationships.

For example, to go back to the issues of property rights and the environment, property rights could include the right to pollute the air from your factory's chimney and dump chemicals in the water that runs through your property. Or we could say, as historically the common law of property did, that the individual rights of property holders are constrained by the rights of other property holders, and by collective goods like clean air. So, rights can shape relations of responsibility, or, of power without responsibility. An approach to rights that always asks the question, How is this definition of a right—say, of property or of free speech—shaping relations? That then leads to the question, What values are at stake? And what kind of structure of relations will promote the values we really care about?

Now of course one can do this kind of analysis and consider only values understood in traditionally individualistic terms. One could focus, for example, on the right to do what one wants with one's property, with a minimum of constraints in the name of freedom; or one can bring in the protection of the vulnerable and the centrality of care to all humans flourishing as integral to the very definition of a right, so not in tension and in contrast to be balanced against rights, but rather built into the meaning of the right. It's important to see that the kind of rights people care about, even from a traditional point of view, require a structure of relations. For example, for free speech to flourish requires a collective culture where people value free expression and encourage it and protect it. No one can enjoy free speech just on their own as an isolated individual. It can only be enjoyed within a structure of relations that fosters it. Most rights really cannot be enjoyed without a supporting structure. Property rights require widespread respect for the idea of private property. People must accept the relations the private property organizes if property is to be secure. I think we can see around the world what happens when one sees those relationships of power and hierarchy are no longer justifiable. People aren't going to respect the underpinning of rights that support that structure of hierarchy.

It's also important to see that to ask these questions about relationships and wider values like care is not to abandon the importance of rights to individuals. This goes to the second question: Why are these still rights? To ask these relational questions is not to say that the collective or the community, and certainly not the state, takes precedence over the individual; that's in essence destroying the meaning of individual rights. On the contrary, seeing that rights structure relationships also helps us to see that people cannot enjoy their individual rights without the structure of relationships that enables that enjoyment. The attention to relationships will do a better job of protecting core values, like equality and liberty for all individuals, by seeing how those values are inseparable from the relationships that sustain them.

The question a relational approach asks are, first: What are the values? Then: What structures of relations will foster those values? And finally: What definition of right, of a given right that's at stake, will foster those relations? I think these questions are completely consistent with existing legal structures. Right now we can encourage judges, lawyers, and ordinary people to always have these kinds of questions in mind when they think about rights.

CARTABIA: Thank you, Jennifer. Let me stress again, once again, you have a better, richer understanding of human experience. You never contrast the individual with the community. You never contrast between rights, between rights and needs. You always try to bring into the definition of rights all the richness of our human experience, which is something very important. Reflecting on my experience, when you were speaking, I was thinking about the cases that arrive on the benches. I think that there is a big enough room to take into consideration the kind of analysis that you propose. Rights are usually defined in very essential terms. Everybody has the right to life, everybody has the right to free speech. The meaning of this right is expounded by judges, and this in turn reflects the common opinion. It is a work that calls for the responsibility of everybody, because also in the judicial rooms we very often have the feeling that we are speaking the voice of the people and of the culture that is commonly shared in society.

John, in one of your books you speak about rights, and the relationship between rights and religion. In our time, rights proliferate as we have seen, and this proliferation has caused a clash of rights. In particular, many of the new rights—for example, reproductive rights, the right to die, right to medical assisted procreation, and many others—are in tension with freedom of religion, which is indeed a basic and important right itself. As a result, in the common opinion, in the public opinion, individual rights and religion are often considered antagonistic.

Let's take an example from the recent facts in Paris: the terrorist attack on *Charlie Hebdo*. Most commentators have described the problem as a conflict between religion and freedom of expression. On the one side, freedom of expression without boundaries, with no limits, everybody can say whatever he or she wants even if it offends people. On the other side, really just a violent reaction to the freedom of expression. *Charlie Hebdo* simply mocked; the writers used the publication as an expression of this idea. We want to defend freedom with no limits. However, some voices have spoken against this understanding and this account. For example, two days ago, Pope Francis said that we have to preserve freedom of expression, but it does not include the freedom to offend other religions and other people. Even in the New York Times, David Brooks said that hate speech is a limit to freedom of expression. So: Why can we consider rights and religion as friends rather than antagonists? Moreover, what kind of relationship do you figure out for a fruitful coexistence between religion and state-protected rights?

WITTE: There's no question that every human right exists in a community of other rights, as Professor Nedelsky has underscored. This has to be done with sensitivity to the relationship that one has with one's neighbor. No right is absolute; every right has to be balanced by the countervailing concerns of other parties. Religious rights deserve to be protected, but they are not absolute as well.

I start with that premise. I also start with a basic notion that we need to get past the schoolboy and schoolgirl ideas we all were taught, that human rights emerged in a post-religious, post-Christian, post-Westphalian settlement, when we finally got over patriarchy and paternalism and abuse and discrimination and we finally put into place a secular rights regime. And the rights regime that obtains in the twentieth and twenty-first century happily is free from religious taint. We may or may not begrudgingly accord rights of religious freedom, but then those rights of religious freedom must necessarily take a back seat to countervailing rights, as the judge in Cartabia's question illustrates.

I'd like to make the argument that religion needs to be a fundamental part of rights conversation, that religious rights need robust protection. Not absolute, but nonetheless on a par with other competing rights claims. I say that for a number of reasons. First of all, without religion, many rights are cut from their roots. Georg Jellinek, the great German jurist, put it a century ago: the right to religion is "the mother of many other rights." For the religious individual, the right to believe leads ineluctably to the rights to speak, to assemble, to worship, to parent, to educate, to travel, and to do a number of things on the strength of those rights. For the religious association, the right to exist invariably involves the rights to corporate property, to organized structure, to freedom of contract, the freedom of press, the ability to gather the institutions that are endemic and appropriate to the exercise of that group right. To ignore religious rights is in many ways to cut our rights from their conceptual and, as I said earlier, their historical root.

Secondly, without religion in human rights discourse, many rights become infinitely expandable. Religious communities, Christians amongst them, press rights because of the need to have the freedom to discharge the religious duties of the faith. Rights and duties belong together, and to separate them is in many ways, in the eyes of many religious communities, disastrous. Rights without duties to guide them quickly become claims of self-indulgence, and duties without rights to exercise them quickly become sources of deep guilt. Religious communities, as part of a discourse of right, keep that combination of rights and duties together.

Third thing. Without religion, the state is often given an exaggerated role to play as the guarantor of human rights. The simple statement versus individual dialectic that obtains in modern discourse of human rights leaves it to the state to vindicate rights of every sort. But the reality is the state simply is not, and cannot be, omni-competent, as the fantastic failures of the communist experiments of the 20th century underscore for us anew. The reality is that between the state and the individual lie a whole series of mediating structures—intermediate associations, we sometimes call them; and religious communities are a critical part of those. Religious communities play a vital role in the realization and the articulation of, and the defense of, first-generation rights of speech and press and assembly.

Religious communities provide important, and are sometimes the only, places to vindicate second-generation rights of education and welfare, artistic opportunities, the basic needs of life. In transitional communities, especially in times of crisis, religious communities often provide zones of liberty, incubators of democracy, to be able to provide—notwithstanding, the destruction of the state, or the excesses of the state, or the tyranny of the state—opportunities for humans to flourish with rights being protected and vindicated.

Finally, without religion, human rights have no enduring narratives to ground them. Human rights norms need a human rights culture, and human rights cultures depend upon concrete values to give them real concrete manifestation. We need basic values of restraint and respect, of accountability and responsibility, which religious communities help to achieve. So my argument is in part that a human rights regime needs religion in order to survive. Otherwise, it's an abstract set of ideals and norms that simply cannot be vindicated. Now the particulars of the tragedies of Paris, the particulars of watching religious communities having their rights claims abused by the rights regime—clearly is a danger point in the inclusion of religion as a vital rights player. To give religious communities religious rights is to court the risk of the rights bearer turning those rights into instruments of the destruction of their neighbor. That simply is a limitation that has to be imposed upon the exercise of religious rights. Life and limb are left to the state through our contractarian philosophy, under due process constraints. To take from another, and to equip a religious community with the power over life and limb is in many ways to betray the most fundamental aspects of the division of responsibility that we have. When religious rights clash with countervailing personal rights, the hard part is what the Holy Father said: finding the way of striking the prudential balances and recognizing that the right to operate doesn't necessarily make it the right thing to do in the circumstances. Perhaps rights absolutism by religious or non-religious groups alike is dangerous to the polity. Finding a rights culture that makes it inherently impossible for a person to think of [abusing others' claims] as an appropriate way to exercise her or his rights or their rights as a group—I think that is one of the things we have to strive for.

CARTABIA: Thank you. Having heard how much your scholarship so far has contributed to a better understanding of human rights now, I'm very curious about your future projects. What are you working on? What might be your future books? What research are you undertaking that may bring fresh air to our reflection and maybe to other topics?

NEDELSKY: Actually, my new project leaves the language of rights behind, and is intended to be a really accessible book. *Laws Relations* was supposed to be an accessible book but my son tells me I didn't quite succeed at that, yeah. [*audience laughter*] It wasn't meant only for academics, but this next one is really meant to be popular. I'm thinking of calling it *Part Time for All*. It's aimed at getting everyone to think about the structure of work and of care. But they really want to define their lives. I think we're facing a crisis that arises out of dysfunctional norms of both work and care. And it takes three forms: one is unsustainable stress on families; the second is persistent inequality for women and for the other subordinated groups who are asked to do the care work that make our lives possible and valuable; and the third is that we have policymakers who by and large are ignorant about the care that life requires. The people who have lots of experience doing care rarely rise to high positions of power. And those in such positions, or on their way up to them, think it's a waste of their time to do their own care work. So, I think these problems require fundamental change in the norms of care and work.

My suggestion is that everybody engage in paid work at least 12 hours and no more than 30 hours a week. Similarly, everyone, no matter how important you are, no matter how special your skills are—everyone engage in care work at least 12 hours a week, up to 30 hours a week. Now what I'm talking about are norms, not laws, not based on rights claims, but about the mutuality of care that is essential to our world. These norms would be strong norms, so just as today most adult men would be embarrassed to tell somebody that they'd never held a job, under my system if you met an adult man who said that he had never spent much time taking care of others, people would wonder what was wrong with him. They might suggest something—a group, a doctor, something to help him figure out why he is so mistaken in what matters in life. Right now it's practically a marker of how important you are that other people do all the care work for you and your family. Under my system, people would no more think about electing a person who was ignorant of the practical demands and rewards of care work than they would elect someone who had never held a job. Both people would be seen as ignorant of core dimensions of human life. So in my short book I'm going to be arguing that only a radical transformation of how we do our work and our care can solve the problems of our stressed families, persistent inequality, and ignorant policymakers.

CARTABIA: Thank you, very well. [*audience applause*] So John, which one of your many projects would you like to speak about? Because I know that there are a number of them.

WITTE: There are three things that people will die for: their faith, their freedom, and their family. And that's what I study. I studied historically, I studied comparatively, I studied it as an inter-religious trope in discussing this with Jews and Christians and Muslims, and increasingly with Asian religions as well. I do it also as an inter-denominational opportunity for deep discussion between Catholics, Protestants, and Orthodox.

One of the projects I'm working on is the question of Church, state, and the institutions in life ,where we have spiritual and temporal dimensions that are in constant tension. There are three big institutions that are at issue. One is the family, a second is the school, and a third is the social welfare institution. Each of them has spiritual and temporal dimensions. Each of them has contested jurisdiction between the Church and the state or religious communities, and political authorities, and each of them now is a deeply contested terrain. Professor Cartabia's question last time, about that tension between religious freedom and sexual liberty, is one little area that introduces the whole set of contrasts between the claims that the religious community makes and the political community makes on a fundamental area of sex, marriage, and family life. We are now in the business of trying to renegotiate that. As the states' understanding of marriage and family has become thinner and thinner and more plastic, religious communities increasingly want out. They want the freedom to be able to exercise their own semi-autonomy for their voluntary faithful over these fundamental questions of sex, marriage, and family.

How much economy do we give them? We've negotiated that in the education field over a long period of time. In contested cases from the 19th and the 20th centuries in America, with the lodestar case of Pierce vs. the Society of Sisters,ultimately deciding that education of children can be shared between religious communities and the state community. We now have worked out a public and private education system with licensing controlling what the private educators do. That is an interesting prototype in which to rethink questions of marriage and family and their governance. The areas of social welfare and charity were just beginning, with faith-based initiatives and other things to rethink the hermetic wall of separation between Church and state that historically obtained in the area of charity, and to let these two systems work separately. The question becomes whether we can renegotiate those boundaries in the 21st century and try to figure out what that looks like, both at the theoretical and constitutional level, but then also at the practical level on the ground. That's one of the projects.

CARTABIA: Thank you, John. Thank you very much. [*audience applause*]

Before concluding this very interesting and enriching conversation, let me stress once again three points I consider a common shared proposition of the members of the panel including myself. First of all, we do not need, and we do not want, to abandon the rights, the individual rights. They are still the cornerstone of our society, and we want them to continue to be this cornerstone. Nevertheless, the second proposition we need is to test rights and rights practice continually—an ongoing test and probably a never-ending test, in order to safeguard the experience of rights as a real human experience of people as an embodiment, as a network, and as a relational human being and not just an individual.

In order to preserve them from becoming a sort of the last utopia, John Witte reminds us that the role of religion is to preserve rights from the excess of an over-expectation. Rights cannot fill out, they have a limited capacity to fulfill human expectation. We do not have to run the risk of demanding too much from rights. The third point which was very clear in our conversation, is that there is something beyond law. There are moral norms, there is culture, there is something that shapes also our legislation and our legal culture.

For example, I think that all the volunteers here in these rooms are giving a great contribution to a different understanding of our life, and to contrast the selfishness that sometimes is such a risk in our Western society. So thank you, everybody. Thank you to our speakers, thank you.

NEW YORK

POTTS
NOWAK
LANDI
MILLER

Martin Nowak, Harvard University

The Emergence of the Human Face

*A presentation with **Kenneth Miller**, Professor of Biology, Brown University, **Martin Nowak**, Professor of Biology and Mathematics, Harvard University, and **Richard Potts**, Director of the Human Origins Program at the Smithsonian, moderated by **Maria Teresa Landi**, Senior Investigator at the National Institutes of Health (NIH), on the degree to which evolution explains who we are*

Introduction

We live in a time when reason tends to be reduced to its scientific-mathematical capabilities, and human nature to its biological component. For example, Sir Francis Crick, co-discoverer of the double-helix structure of the DNA molecule, wrote at the beginning of The Astonishing Hypothesis (1994): "The Astonishing Hypothesis is that 'You,' your joys and your sorrows, your memories and your ambitions, your sense of personal identity and your free will, are in fact no more than the behavior of a vast assembly of nerve cells and their associated molecules."

But...is that reasonable? What are the features that define human beings? Can evolution explain human nature? How does biological evolution work in the first place? These are some questions that the speakers will address.

MARIA TERESA LANDI: Good afternoon, and welcome. My name is Maria Teresa Landi. I am a scientist at the National Institutes of Health, and the moderator of this panel on the emergence of the human face. I'm delighted to introduce today three renowned speakers who will guide us through the foundations of biological evolution and, specifically, to

Saturday, January 17, 2015

the evolutionary journey that led to the emergence of human beings. We human beings are aware of our connection with the animal world, and yet our experience tells us that we are unique; it is important, therefore, to ask what science can tell us about this connection with the animal world—but also what lies beyond the boundaries of the scientific method.

We've asked the speakers today to guide us through the principals and mechanisms of evolution, with their relevance and limitations in offering a definition of man. As Pope Benedict XVI once said, to evolve means, literally, to roll a scroll; that is, to read a book. It is a book whose history was evolution, whose writing and meaning we read according to the different approaches of the sciences.

Today we have with us scientists who represent three such approaches. Doctors Ken Miller, a cell biologist; Martin Nowak, a mathematician; and Rick Potts, a paleoanthropologist.

I think we can begin with Professor Miller. Kenneth Miller is Professor of Biology at Brown University. A cell biologist, he serves as an advisor on life sciences to the NewsHour, a PBS television program on news and public affairs, and is a Fellow of the American Association for the Advancement of Science. Miller is co-author with Joseph Levine of a series of high school and college biology textbooks used by millions of students nationwide.

In 2005 he served as lead witness in the Kitzmiller vs. Dover trial on evolution and intelligent design in Pennsylvania. His popular book, *Finding Darwin's God, a Scientist's Search for Common Ground Between God and Evolution*, addresses the scientific status of evolutionary theory and its relationship to religious views of nature. His latest book, *Only a Theory: Evolution and the Battle for America's Soul*, addresses the continuous struggle over how evolution is to be understood in American society.

You can find in the New York Encounter program a huge, impressive list of honors that Professor Miller has received. I just want to mention here that, in 2011, the Society for the Study of Evolution recognized Dr. Miller with the Stephen Jay Gould Prize for advancing the public understanding of evolution. And, more recently, in 2014 Notre Dame University honored him with a presentation of the Laetare Medal.

So, Ken—we hear a lot about evolution; and particularly when it relates to the evolution of man, there is quite a hot debate between different sides. Yet the impression is that there is confusion as to what evolution is really about, and often this debate is not well-grounded in facts. So can you tell us some elements of the foundations and fundamentals of Darwin's laws of evolution, and how they are also scientific demonstrations.

KENNETH MILLER: Well, I will do my best. And thank you very much for having me here. Human evolution remains a flashpoint in American education and culture, and you don't have to look very far to see examples of things like state legislatures passing laws to promote the teaching of alternatives to evolutionary theory. When the *Cosmos* TV series recently aired on one of the broadcast networks, there was a station in Oklahoma that blacked out one of the episodes and omitted any mention of evolution. I think the reasons for concern about evolution, particularly relevant to this group, are clearly religious in nature, and they play into the stereotype of "science versus faith."

I can't tell you how many times in public talks I've been asked the very question that you see on that church slide: If man evolved from monkeys, why are monkeys still here? I want to tell you how I answer that. I tell the person, "I'll answer that in a second, but first, I have a question for you: Where did Protestants come from?"

And they look at me a little strange, and I say, "Come on, it was the ninety-three theses, Martin Luther, it was in all the—"

"Oh!" They say, "I guess Protestants came from Catholics."

"Are Catholics still here? There's the answer to why monkeys are still here." [*audience laughter, clapping*]

And if you'd like to bring this up in a contemporary way, Texas was actually the latest—not the only, but the latest—battleground. And it was a battle over a single textbook that had such as strong treatment of evolution that the Texas Board of Education deferred its approval. I'll show you the cover of this horrible textbook right here. If you look closely, you will see my name on the cover. It was, in fact, my textbook that was held up. Once it was sent out for expert review, it was clear that, in fact, it gave a very strong, coherent, and correct treatment of evolution, and now is widely used in the great state of Texas, something for which I and my co-author are very proud.

I'll give you another example—involving a potential presidential candidate—of how people are concerned about evolution. This is Mike Huckabee, former governor of Arkansas. A couple of years ago when he was asked for his views he said, "If anybody else wants to believe that they are the descendants of a primate, they are certainly welcome to do so." But of course Governor Huckabee does not believe that. I've always wanted to meet Governor Huckabee, and maybe if he runs this year I can go up to New Hampshire, not far from where I live; and if I do, I'll call him aside, I'll tell him I really like a lot of his positions—he's an energetic campaigner, he's a wonderful guy—but Governor Huckabee, you are a primate, and not only that, so were your mom and dad, and so you are most certainly descended from a primate.

He might be tempted to say, "Well, is it Darwin who said that?"

And the answer is, "No, it wasn't Charles Darwin. It was actually a God-fearing creationist named Carolus Linneaus, who in fact was the first person to recognize that human beings are indeed primates."

Now, evolution by natural selection is an astonishingly simple idea. And it rests upon four verifiable premises: one, there's variation in natural populations; two, in every generation, more offspring are produced than can possibly survive to maturity; three, as a result there is a struggle for existence; and four, characteristics that are beneficial in that struggle are going to become more common in a population over time. The conclusion of all this is that, over time and given new variations, this can lead to the emergence of new species.

Now, evolution is actually a lot more complicated than that. I put this slide in not because anybody can read all of the stuff up there, but because this is from a college biology textbook showing a variety of evolutionary mechanisms—not all of which are related to natural selection—that drive evolution. And you'll hear more about these from Martin Nowak.

When we look for evidence of evolution, inevitably we look for fossils. There are many, many ways to show that the statement here by the National Academy is true, which is: we have so many intermediate series that document evolution, it's sometimes difficult to know where one species leaves off and another one begins. A great example of this is the series of fossils documenting the evolution of the first tetrapods, the first land-based, four-legged vertebrates, which we now understand in great detail.

If you'd like to read up about this, there's a wonderful book by the great science writer Carl Zimmer, called *At the Water's Edge*, which talks about two very, very compelling fossil series through which we understand how life moved from the water onto the land. Human evolution tells a similar story, and Rick Potts, who's going to speak at the end of our session, is going to document the details of that. But my work is in cellular and molecular biology, and I have to tell you that the most spectacular evidence of evolution is actually found not so much in fossils but in the human genome itself. In fact, this is an issue of the journal *Nature* from about 10 years ago, in which the lead article basically pointed out that molecular data have spectacularly confirmed Darwin's inference that we share recent common ancestors with the great apes.

I want to give you two quick examples of this, which I think are really compelling. We are placental mammals. All placental mammals, when they develop, when you and I developed as an embryo, form a yolk sac. There's a photograph here of a human embryo, with the yolk sac next to it like a balloon in a drawing from *Grey's Anatomy*. Now, what's peculiar about this is that our yolk sac has no yolk in it. It's empty. So why do our embryos form a yolk sac that encloses absolutely nothing at all? If you looked at design principles it would make no sense, but if you understand that we mammals evolved from animals with the yoke containing eggs, suddenly the presence of that empty yolk sac makes sense, because it's part of our evolutionary developmental history. That's just structure, morphology. But here's the insight. If we descended from creatures that once laid yolky eggs, maybe there are genes for the yolk protein—which is called vitellogenin—lurking somewhere in the human genome, betraying our evolutionary ancestry. We now have the tools to look for that. And guess what—they are there. The human genome actually has three copies of genes for the yolk protein vitellogenin. They're all broken, none of them are functional, but they sit there as a remnant of our evolutionary ancestors. Now the late Stephen Jay Gould once called such things senseless signs of history. They provide proof, as he put it, that the world was not made in its present form and neither were we. We have an evolutionary past. But there's another senseless side of history in our genetics.

We humans have 46 chromosomes. All the other great apes have 48. Why are we missing a pair of chromosomes? Well, the only way to explain it is that the two chromosomes still separate in the other great apes must've accidentally gotten fused in us to form a single chromosome, dropping us to 46. That's a testable explanation. If it's true, then our genome ought to contain the remnants of two chromosomes recently fused together. How would we recognize that? Turns out to be easy. I've sketched two chromosomes here: the tips of every chromosome have very special sequences called telomeres, which I've sketched in in blue. If one of your chromosomes had been formed by the fusion of two chromosomes that very recently were separate, you know what it should look like? It should have telomere DNA right in the center. And it should have two sequences rather than one node of centromeres. Do we have such a chromosome? You bet we do. It's human chromosome number two, and it also betrays our common ancestry with these organisms by virtue of that fusion site. Now for some molecular studies: I put a few representative books up here, including one of my own, that have described this for lay readers. Molecular studies confirm our evolutionary ancestry in our relationship to other organisms.

I want to close by pointing out what I think this means. A distinguished professor of biology, David Barash, University of Washington, wrote a much-cited op-ed in the *New York Times* this year, called "God, Darwin, and My College Biology Class." And he wrote that every year he has "the talk" with his students. The talk isn't about sex or drugs, but about religion and science and how they don't get along. What Dr. Barash wrote was that evolution has demolished pillars of religious faith; in particular because it was an undirected and natural process—not divine creation—that gave rise to us, and he finds this to be antithetical to religious faith.

But I would ask: Is it really a problem to point out that life was generated by purely natural processes? I recall a quote from Saint Augustine that says the universe was brought into being in a less-than-fully-formed state, but was gifted to transform itself from unformed matter into a truly marvelous array of structure and life forms. Augustine would have been at home with the idea that life could be created from the natural world. Barash also wrote that we have no supernatural traits, being made of ordinary molecules. Well, we are, but is it a "problem" to think that we are an ordinary part of the natural world? I read another book once that said, "Remember me, that thou art dust, and to dust thou shalt return." We surely are part of the natural world, and in fact he also wrote that the more we learn of evolution, the more we're drawn to the conclusion that living things are produced by a natural and amoral process. Now it's true that the process of evolution does not require a divine explanation, but we can ask another question, however: Why should nature support the extravagant creativity of the evolutionary process? Science itself has no answer to that question, but faith may see it as the work of the very same creator. In fact, my message to Dr. Barash would be to skip the talk and just focus on biology.

Evolution fully and properly understood does not support the case against God that Dr. Barash wishes to make. In a very real sense, in evolutionary design, life is part of the inherent fabric of the natural world, and the capacity for evolutionary change is built into nature. If you are a believer, this can be understood as part of God's providential plan. A distinguished paleontologist, Simon Conway Morris, expressed this in his wonderful book, *Life's Solutions*, about the convergent properties of evolution and the emergence of humans on this planet.

What I would say in conclusion is that we do not need to find room for God in the evolutionary process, because if God exists, then the process of evolution itself is part of a natural world of His own making. In the Catholic context in particular, this fact has been very clearly stated by three popes: Pius XII, John Paul II, and Benedict XVI, and most recently by a fourth pope, Francis, who is very much a friend of science. Thank you. [*audience applause*]

LANDI: Thank you, Ken. Now we have more clarity on the foundation of this evolution, and in a way you're already introducing the next speaker, Martin Nowak. Martin Nowak is Professor of Biology and Mathematics at Harvard University and Director of the Program for Evolutionary Dynamics. He works on the mathematical theory of evolution, including the evolution of cooperation in human language and the dynamics of virus infections and human cancer. An Austrian by birth, he studied biochemistry and mathematics at the University of Vienna. He then went to the University of Oxford as the Erwin Schrödinger scholar, and became Professor of Mathematical Biology.

In 1998 he moved to Princeton to establish the first program in Theoretical Biology at the Institute for Advanced Study. He received his present position at Harvard University in 2003. A corresponding member of the Austrian Academy of Sciences, Nowak is the recipient of several prizes, including the well-known Memorial Prize of Oxford University, the David Starr Jordan Prize of Stanford University, and the Aikido Kubel Prize of the Society for Mathematical Biology. Nowak is the author of over four hundred papers, and four books. You can read much more about the outstanding work of Martin on the New York Encounter website and also in the program.

So, Martin: in your 2011 book, *The SuperCooperators*, and also in many related articles, you propose that natural selection or genetic variation are not enough to explain reality, by which I mean the reality of evolution. You propose "cooperation" among the forces of evolution. While natural selection—as we have heard from Ken—introduces a conflict, cooperation, means that an individual, if I understand correctly, pays a cost for another individual to receive a benefit. Can you tell us more?

MARTIN NOWAK: Some more, yes. That's the topic of my talk, and I'm very, very happy to be here. I will talk about the evolution of cooperation and why I think that cooperation is a fundamental principle of the living world. I'm a mathematical biologist, and I want to tell you a little story about what that means. There is a shepherd and a flock of sheep. A man comes by and says, If I guess the correct number of sheep in your flock, can I have one? So the shepherd says, Okay, try. The man looks and says,

83. The shepherd is amazed, because that's the right number. So the man picks up a sheep and starts to walk away, but the shepherd says, Hang on: If I guess your profession, can I have my sheep back? And the man says, Please try. The shepherd says, You must be a mathematical biologist. How did you know? Because, the shepherd says, you picked up my dog. [*audience laughter*]

In my field, as you can tell, it's about getting the numbers right, and so today I hope we get the numbers right for the evolution of cooperation. Here, already, are three examples of cooperation. On the one part of the slide, on the left side, you can see filaments of bacteria that already existed three billion years ago. These are individual cells that formed strings like pearls, and every so often a cell dies in order to feed the others with nitrogen. So here we have an extreme form of cooperation, where one cell gives its life in order to feed others.

In the middle of the slide is a kind of cooperation that came into existence 125 million years ago, that of social insects. And in social insects, workers do not reproduce themselves but they help the queen reproduce. Why do they give up their own ability to reproduce in order to help another individual reproduce? It was a question that was asked: If everything is just natural selection, how would we get the design of such an animal? On the right part of the slide is an example from our own evolutionary time, from right now: just two thousand years ago there was the Good Samaritan; this is a painting by Vincent Van Gogh.

People help one another. Why? That's a fundamental question. If everything is just natural selection, if it's just survival of the fittest, why would cells, animals, or people help one another? Here you see an image of the Fukushima power plant and the rescue workers, the first ones called to give help. I can show you a similar image, of course, of the disaster of 9/11 and the rescue response of the firefighters who came in there willing to help. You could ask them, Why are you doing this? When the Fukushima power plant was melting down, a worker in his 20s was amongst those who volunteered to reenter. He knew the choice might prevent him from ever marrying or having children for fear of permanent health consequences. He was asked in an interview why he did this, and he said, There are only some of us who can do this job, and I'm single and young and I feel it's my duty to help solve this problem.

Why do people help one another? Here's another example from this very city. Didn't New York have a hero, the story of the man who was waiting in the subway with his daughters? They were on their way to school. A nearby stranger suddenly suffered a seizure and fell down in front of the train. The train's headlights were already visible as it came into the station, but the father jumped down to the track in order to pull this man up. He then realized it was too late to actually get the man to safety, so he threw himself over the man and protected him as the train went over both of them, leaving them unharmed.

Very few of us would be so heroic as to actually save another person's life, especially at such great personal risk. But all of us, I think, have the remarkable, intuitive, instinctive feeling of, Oh my god, something very dangerous is happening here, what can I do to help? What can I do to help this other person? So the question is, Why do we have this instinct? Why does evolution grip us with such a sense of helping another unrelated individual? Do animals have this? Presumably not. If they see one animal dying, why would they help it? It's a competitor. Why do people have this?

And this has to do with the creation of cooperation. This is a timeline I show to my students at the beginning of every class, so as to put everything into perspective. You can ask the physicists, How old is the universe? And they answer, 13.7 billion years old. How old is the sun, the earth, the moon? About 4.6 billion years old. When was the origin of life? Around four billion years ago on earth, that's the conjecture. But the evidence is that, by 3.5 billion years ago, there was bacterial life on earth, chemical evidence for bacterial life, and that by 1.8 billion years ago there were so-called nucleotic cells, cells with a nucleus, the higher organized cells. By 600 million years ago we have complex multicellular life, and in the last 1,000,000 years, humans, human language.

For me, these are the great steps in the evolutionary process, and my observation is that for these great steps in evolution you actually need cooperation as a kind of master architect. It's not only competition; with competition you get better and better adaptation of the same level of organization, but cooperation is that which brings about more complicated levels of organization. Cooperation brings about the emergence of multi-cellular organisms. Cancer, for example, is a breakdown of cooperation amongst the cells in a multicellular organism. Cooperation brings about social animals, it brings about human species. So what is it that evolves?

Populations of reproducing individuals, the carrier of the evolutionary process is the population of reproducing individuals. Mutation means that new types arise over time, and selection means that different types grow at different rates. So these are the two fundamental forces: mutation and selection. And to this, I would argue, you actually have to add cooperation because only cooperation is that which gives you the emergence of complexity, the shift from simple organization to more complicated organization. In a very simple mathematical sense, cooperation is an interaction between two individual cells or people. There is a donor and there is a recipient, and the donor pays a cost while the recipient gets a benefit.

So again the question is: Why should you help somebody who's a potential competitor? This interaction between two people leads to a very famous game in game theory called the Prisoner's Dilemma. In a moment I want to play this Prisoner's Dilemma with all of you, but here are the rules of the game. You cooperate or you defect, and I cooperate or I defect. And there are only two parameters in this game: the benefit and the cost. The benefit of cooperation and the cost of cooperation. If you cooperate and I cooperate, then you pay the cost because you cooperate; but you have to benefit because I cooperate. So you have B minus C. If I defect and you cooperate, then you only have the cost of your cooperation minus C, but you have no advantage because I did not cooperate. But when you defect and I cooperate, you have plus B; you have no cost, just a benefit from my cooperation. And if we both defect, it's zero.

So, I can put some numbers there. For example, benefit is three, cost is one, and these are the rules of the game. What is written here is a payoff matrix, and in the payoff matrix I have specified what you will get. You have to decide now whether you want to cooperate or whether you want to defect.

We will decide simultaneously.

If you want to cooperate with me, raise your hand. Who wants to defect? I should say it's not an optional game, you know. We have optional games also where you have a third possibility of doing nothing, but here you have only two choices: cooperation or defection.

So let me ask again, Who wants to cooperate? Who wants to defect? This is the most cooperative society I have ever seen. [*audience laughter*] The only more-cooperative society I have seen was in Beijing, where there was an audience of 2,000. Nobody defected. But mostly New York is pretty cooperative, you know, so this is how you should analyze the game.

You don't know what I will do. Let's assume I cooperate. If you cooperate, you have two points. But if you defect, you have three points. What is better, three or two? Three is better than two, so if I cooperate, it's better for you to defect. If I defect, you have a choice between zero and minus one. Zero is better than minus one, so if I defect it's also better for you to defect. No matter what I do, it's better for you to defect. If I analyze the game in the same way, we both get zero.

And that's bad, because it would have been better had we both cooperated, because then we would get two. This is the Nash equilibrium analysis of the game. The Nash equilibrium here is to defect. So, the dilemma is that two so-called rational players—in the sense of game theory—defect and end up with a low payoff; but two irrational players might cooperate and receive a higher payoff.

Cooperation is irrational, but human experiments show that people are not necessarily rational. They behave in a way that indicates a wish cooperate, even though in a given situation it might not make sense. If you're familiar with the field of mathematics called Game Theory, then you know it was invented by Oskar Morgenstern and John von Neumann, a Hungarian who at Princeton also built the first programmable computer. Interesting thing is, you don't need to call on rationality here to explain the defection; it's chosen also by natural selection: in a population where there's random cooperation and defectors meeting each other, defectors always have an advantage, they always get a higher payoff. For natural selection to favor cooperation over defection, you need to provide some help. And this help is key in terms of mechanisms for the evolution of cooperation. These mechanisms also explain why you, here, predominantly wanted to cooperate in this game, because the human intuition is a cooperative one.

There are five mechanisms for the evolution of cooperation: Direct Reciprocity, Indirect Reciprocity, Special Selection, Group Selection, and Kin Selection. I will very briefly discuss these mechanisms. They form the environment where natural selection shaped the intuition that people have of why they want to cooperate. Direct Reciprocity means: I help you, you help me. The idea is, we play a repeated game, and in the repeated game it makes sense to cooperate, because we can establish a relationship that is mutually beneficial.

Human cooperation is not only explained by Direct Reciprocity, there's also Indirect Reciprocity. The Good Samaritan did not think in terms of a repeated game; he didn't think, I'll cooperate and then later this person will help me. There's something else going on, and this is what we call Indirect Reciprocity. I help you, somebody helps me; if I'm in that situation, I wish somebody would come by here to help me. Indirect Reciprocity works by a reputation; we are always acting in a way, conscious of the idea that others might observe us. My friend David Haig at Harvard said for Direct Reciprocity you need a face. For Indirect Reciprocity you need a name. Indirect Reciprocity has to do with people talking to each other about others. It has to do with elevation of the Internet, it has to do with trust.

Special Selection is the idea that neighbors help each other, forming clusters of helpful people who can survive in a competitive, exploitative world. In social networks you help each other, you help your friend, and you form a community of friendship.

Group Selection is really an idea that goes back to Charles Darwin. He said, "There can be no doubt that a tribe with many members ready to give aid to each other and to sacrifice themselves for the common good, would be victorious over other tribes; and this would be natural selection." The idea is that you have competition between groups of people, and in one group people help each other, and that group is favored over a group where people do not help each other.

Finally, Kin Selection is interaction occurring between genetic relatives. "I will jump into the river to save two brothers or eight cousins," was a statement made by J.B.S. Haldane, a founding father of population genetics. You help those who are genetically your relatives. And so I talked about these five mechanisms: Direct Reciprocity, Indirect Reciprocity, Special Selection, Group Selection, and Kin Selection. They are intellectual structures that help natural selection to favor cooperation over competition. But, in an interesting observation of my work on such games and interactions over the last 20 or more years, what I've found is that winning strategies have these three properties: they are generous, hopeful, and forgiving. Generous in the sense that you don't necessarily demand always the larger share of the pie. Sometimes you're willing to accept a deal where the other person gets more than you, but you have a good interaction. Hopefully, this means than whenever you see a stranger you start this cooperation, you hope to establish a cooperative relationship. Forgiving means that in the repeated interaction, if somebody defects against you, you forgive; you can move beyond this and you can start this cooperation again. And these are properties of winning strategies in these mechanisms.

Finally, I should say that right now we are faced with the biggest problem of cooperation ever, and this is the question, really: How do we establish cooperation on a global level in order to solve the climate problem? This also includes how to cooperate with future generations, because we want to leave them a world that has an ecosystem habitable for the human species. We should be paying a cost now so that future generations have a benefit. Right now we are doing the opposite: we are actually burdening them with debt. We're spending their money now and they can pay it back later. We are destroying the environment and they should repair it later—that's actually a problem. We have to shift from this defection with the future to actual cooperation with the future.

Some of the ideas I mentioned today are in two books. One is called *SuperCooperators*, a biology book. Then, another that I wrote with a Professor of Divinity at Harvard University, now at Cambridge University, on the discussion of evolution cooperation in Christianity. Thank you very much. [*audience applause*]

LANDI: This is getting really, really interesting, and we'll ask Rick to illustrate this with pictures, but let me first introduce him. Richard Potts is a paleoanthropologist, Director of the Smithsonian Human Origins Program, and Curator of Anthropology at the National Museum of Natural History. Since joining the Smithsonian in 1985, Rick has dedicated his research to piecing together the record of Earth's environmental change and human adaptation. His ideas on how human evolution responded to environmental instability have stimulated wide attention and new research in several scientific fields. Rick has developed international collaborations among scientists interested in the ecological aspects of human evolution. He leads excavations at early human sites in the East African Rift Valley, including the famous hand-axe site of Olorgesailie, Kenya, and Kanam, near Lake Victoria, Kenya.

He also co-directs ongoing projects in southern and northern China that compare evidence of early human behavior and environments from eastern Africa to eastern Asia. He received his PhD in Biological Anthropology from Harvard University in 1982, after which he taught anthropology at Yale University and served as Curator of Physical Anthropology at the Yale Peabody Museum. Rick is Curator of the David Koch Hall of Human Origins at the Smithsonian's Natural History Museum, and author of the companion book, *What Does it Mean to be Human?*

So, Rick: we've heard the basic foundations of biological evolution and the theory of cooperation. You've participated in the excavations of early human sites. Can you illustrate with some pictures what you and others have found in the caves of your excavations, and help us understand how biological evolution played a role in the origin of humanity?

RICHARD POTTS: I'd be happy to. Good afternoon, everyone, it's a delight to be here. I thought, given that the theme of this session is the emergence of the human face, I would start in a very literal sense with human faces, or with the faces of ancestors and relatives of ours, who science joined together with our own species, *Homo sapiens*, as part of our unique, evolutionary branch in the tree of life.

The pictures are all of ourselves, they all have different scientific names. The names sometime read like characters in a Russian novel. You don't have to memorize them all, but they do represent ways of life that united in their own way, some combination of the features of what it means to be human, what in a biological sense we think of as uniquely human traits. As far as we know, all of them, like all other primates, were highly social, lived in social groups, and over the last two and a half million years some of them made tools, mainly tools of stone. They, many of them, had large brains, and some of them— the Neanderthals, for example, which are featured in the upper right-hand corner of the screen—even had a symbolic sense, or at least the roots of a symbolic sense.

They're known to have made occasional art objects, modifications of the environment that seem to have no specific function, and occasionally buried their dead with grave goods, such as colorful flowers. Yet despite these fractions, many of which correspond to what it means to be biologically human today, none of these species are on earth any longer. They all have met their demise and that is, I think, one of the most profound and provocative aspects of understanding our evolutionary history.

Now we used to think of the species as forming a linear arrangement leading to us, and this was a narrative of human origins that had a sense of inevitability to it, an arrangement connoting progress inevitably leading to ourselves. And, of course, this kind of art has become an icon of cultural progress that you see in magazines and newspapers and even in advertisements. In fact, this happens to be my favorite. Somehow [audience laughter] leading to perfection, a Guinness beer. That will be later.

We no longer think this, but rather instead we see ourselves, in this particular representation, as being at the top of a tree where it says, "You are here," with faces indicating the diversity of humanity today—but all within one species: we're part of a diverse and branching array of species, all related to us, even though they do not exist today. And so our evolutionary tree is seen as diverse and branching, much like the evolutionary trees of virtually all other organisms. Now, how do we know this? We know this through the fossil record, but we can also consider a different concept of the human face, and that's the way of life that we know as being human today.

At the bottom of the slide, going back to three and a half million years ago, we have the famous series of footprints discovered by Dr. Mary Leakey, that are embedded in volcanic ash in northern Tanzania. We see the arc of skulls and bipedality—our ability to walk upright is one of the first keynote traits, one of the first milestones along the path that define the origin of all of those species that are part of our evolutionary tree. The arc of five skulls that you see there are just a few of the skulls representing two-and-a-half million years of human evolution, and show changes from the bottom left to the right, where we see a skull of our own species, *Homo sapiens*. These changes in brain size and face size took place over time. The skull representing our own species, on the bottom right—you'll notice we're the only mammal whose face is tucked under the brain case. The faces of all the other, earlier human species were in front of the brain case.

That's a physical mark of what is uniquely human about our species, as seen by paleoanthropologists, anatomists, and so on. But then in the upper left one can see a few objects representing two-and-a-half million years of changes in the objects people made, changes in our ability to alter the environment, and to make things—from simple choppers to hand-axes, that oval object in the middle, and then around thirty-two, thirty-three thousand years ago the earliest known sewing needles made out of ivory and bone. Those particular ones come from China. And then the explosion of art: what I'll show in a few minutes is some of the earliest evidence yet found of using color in a way that is seen to represent, to be emblematic of, the origin of the human being as understanding symbolism—to be able to create color, and to understand and express group identity.

The human fossil record a hundred years ago was basically a few dozen fossils, mainly those of Neanderthals in Europe, but now there are over 6,000 fossil individuals representing the last six million years of human evolutionary history. Some of them are nearly complete or quite complete skeletons, while others are just isolated teeth. Added to these, however, are tens of thousands of archaeological remains that are echoes of the behavior of those ancestors and relatives of ours. Not just the ability to make tools, but the ability to make fire, to interact with the environment in ways that transformed the ability of humans to persist in a changing world. And so we can see in this slide a timeline of human evolutionary history. It's a pretty complex slide.

If you can see the numbers starting at six million at the bottom, and then near the present at the top, you'll notice that the advent, the emergence, the accumulation of features, was not all at once but rather an accumulation over time, where various things were added, from walking upright, to changes in diet, to the ability to flake stone, and the roots of being able to modify the environment—these go back to two-and-a-half million years ago. The greatest rate of increase in brain size occurred over the last 800,000 to one million years. And with this came the ability to traverse long distances, to have changes in technology, the emergence of fire and home bases, places that the group members return to over and over again, the ability to transport material and to exchange it over long distances with distant groups, perhaps indicative of the initial sense of cooperation, not just with members of our own group but with others a distance away. Then our symbolic abilities, much more recent in time, and then the diversification of cultures, and of histories, the splintering of the human experience, but based upon these changes that become part of the universal story of our origins. This story, this narrative belongs to every person—not only those in this room, but those living all over the earth today.

Now sometimes I point out to audiences that my research combines the two least-controversial areas of science in American society—evolution and climate change. [*audience laughter*] And we see with the study of climate change that the evolutionary venture, our evolutionary venture, took place in an era of enormous environmental challenge and uncertainty. And so this is a fairly complicated slide. It goes from three million years ago on the right, to the present on the left, and this is something that has become known as African climate dynamics or climate variability. Just in the last ten years, in fact, I published a series of articles—well I'm in the process of publishing a series of articles, the first of which came out last year—which show that the time period of human origins in Africa had this alternating sense of high variability, a great instability of environment followed by stability.

Instability followed by stability, through time. You can get a sense of this on the slide, but mathematically this can be shown, and the explanations are known from looking at astronomical cycles that help control the climate conditions of earth. And what we have found in the analysis of human evolution, when put into this environmental context, is that the key transitions in human evolution, the origins, the earliest known origins of our species, *Homo sapiens*, but also the development of each of the key stone technologies over time, all of the major extinctions and geographic dispersal events—all of these occurred, based on our current evidence, in the most prolonged periods of high climate variability, of climate instability. So climate instability seems to have been this cutting-edge border between thriving and declining, between survival and extinction in the era of human origins. We have this metaphor that perhaps you've heard, that East Africa or Africa is the cradle of human evolution. I now tend to think of it as the cauldron of human evolution, reflecting the roiling events and churning processes that typified the time period of our evolutionary origin. After several million years, we're the sole survivors of that diversification of bipedal species. We're the only ones left. *Homo sapiens*, worldwide in extent, are really a turning point in the history of life, due to our evolved capacity to survive in a changing world.

Let me just show you very briefly some of our recent finds. These are not yet published, but I know this small group can keep a secret. In our excavations in the Rift Valley of southern Kenya, where we are able to look at places like eroded hillsides and gullies, where rain and water have exposed artifacts and fossilized bones on the ground, we come in and excavate what nature has already begun to expose. We find these things, these objects. We have in this particular site, where I've led excavations for the last thirty years, seven hundred thousand years of stone hand-axes, one layer after another, of stone hand-axes.

But there's a change that occurs between 500,000 and 320,000 years ago. Just 320,000 years ago is part of the beginning of one of these prolonged periods of high climate oscillation. What we see is a smaller, more diverse, more mobile technology; the beginning of human innovation. We have careful ways of preparing rocks, such that with one strike of the rock you get over and over again these triangular points. These are the earliest known projectile points, things that fly through the air. The world hasn't been the same since.

We also find the earliest evidence of pigments, of coloring material. Again, emblematic of the symbolic sense of creating group identity. We also have many of those objects there that are obsidian, and were actually traded with groups about 100 kilometers away. Groups that cannot be seen, but are kept in mind by others. We have an element of our humanity that allows us to imagine a value system that one can trade with a group a long distance away. What we see, then, is a huge turnover, a change in the animals that were also there in the Rift Valley of Africa. The extinction of large-bodied grazing elephants, hippos, pigs, baboons, and zebras, and the emergence of the kinds of animals you would see if you were on safari in East Africa.

What we have are these innovations near the origin of *Homo sapiens.* The timeline at the bottom is about 300,000 years long. We see the first evidence of *Homo sapiens* fossils about 200,000 years ago, and over time we see innovations in being able to traverse long distances, in developing a symbolic sense, and so on. All of these occurred in a period of very prolonged climate oscillation: this increasing innovation, the wider social networks, complex symbolic activity, in evidently indicating language and also complex thinking and planning—all of these have to do with a greater capacity to adjust to new environments. We used to see adaptation in human evolution as occurring on an unchanging stage. A stage that may have looked something like this: you put these early bipeds out on an African savanna, and there were dangers that ultimately led to our lineage overcoming these dangers, dominating them, and having dominion over them. But now we have a new narrative of human evolution, based on environmental records fused with the study of human evolution.

It's not a story of adaptation to one single ancestral environment, but rather the opening up, the liberation of human beings from any one ancestral setting. Of having a malleability of culture and language, in being symbolic. This is a story of adaptability, not inevitability. And it leads to a question as I go back to this evolutionary tree on the screen. The provocative question is, "Are we it?" This question used to make us wonder, used to make us wonder: Are human beings the end of creation? Are we the pinnacle of evolution? But now I think we must be quite humble in the face of a different meaning, a far more poignant meaning to that question. We are the last of that radiation of species, we are the last biped standing, so to speak. And so the question, "Are we it?" invites us to examine, not just to react to, but really, truly, and deeply explore how humanity can possibly thrive, change, and adjust in a future that continues to be a changing world. And with this new kind of question comes astonishing responsibilities toward understanding our place in the world, and our deep impact on it. Thank you. [*audience applause*]

LANDI: Thank you, Rick. We have heard about cooperation, about symbolic language—all of these elements that define human beings. But the question I really want to ask is: To what extent does biological evolution, as we've heard discussed here today, explain what man is? When I say man, I mean me, you, our perception of ourselves, our longing for beauty, for happiness, the fight for ideals, for justice, for freedom—how much of this is explained by biological evolution? I'll start with you, Rick.

POTTS: Okay, sure, that's an easy one, isn't it? [*audience laughter*] Well, science and those researchers motivated to explore and understand our evolutionary history really have very little basis for claiming that a human, the human, is solely about anatomy, is solely about our physical appearance. And I've tried to explain a little bit in my talk about how we dig, we uncover things, fossilized remains, stone tools and those echoes of behavior that go beyond the mere physical. We dig up these things that were once buried in darkness and that shed light on the roots our existence as living, ever-changing, ever-challenged beings. And I think this connects with those elements of our humanity that are not specifically explained by changes in genes.

I recently read Anthony Doerr's novel, *All the Light We Cannot See*. Perhaps some of you have read it. Toward the end of the book there's a wonderful reflection on the human brain. It refers to the human brain as one wet kilogram within which spanned universes. Now that's a paraphrase, and our brains actually are a bit more than one kilogram in weight. But it contains and creates intricate universes and meanings that go beyond the material structure of the brain. Our neuroanatomy joined with the social brain, the social networks of which we are a part, create astonishing narratives and meanings. Therefore is our existence, through an understanding of biological evolution, simply a physical manifestation? No one I know who studies the archaeology of human origins would ever say that.

Instead, in the pigments that I showed, which seem to indicate the roots of our symbolic selves, I see the beginning of what we might call, metaphorically, the human face. Those rare and valuable pieces of obsidian traded with groups 100 kilometers away connote the beginning of awareness, of a consciousness about other people, people who cannot be seen in your immediate social group. In those tiny, innocent artifacts I see the emergence of what metaphorically we might call the human face.

The human face is something more then its physicality, something more than its physical appearance, and the study of evolution actually discloses this fact and helps us document it. It exposes the ancient timing of transformations in human nature, and especially the emergence of our cultural nature, from which music and beauty and a variety of other concepts and histories emerge. I think that evolution helps us, the study of it helps us understand the reality of those elements of our humanity that set the stage for seeing things and powers unseen, and for remembering histories and for developing faith. While some people may put huge barriers between science and reason, and faith and reason, I see no conflict.

LANDI: Thank you. I was impressed when you quoted the novel: one kilogram is more than the entire universe. It reminded me of the famous Pascal definition, which says that one single man is worth more than the entire universe, because he's aware of himself and the universe. What do you think?

MILLER: Well, what I'm always struck by is the dualism that has often been part of Western culture, and I don't just mean mind-body dualism, but the tendency to set ourselves apart from the rest of the living world. We are indeed something special, but the notion that we are somehow fundamentally different from nature implies that we evolved out of nature. I prefer to say that we evolved with nature, that we are part of the natural world. I'm often approach by my students when I teach my introductory biology class at the university, and I go through DNA, RNA, the Krebs cycle, biochemistry, the transmission of nerve impulses and so forth, and occasionally I'm asked a question which says, Do you mean that we are nothing but collections of molecules, or mere molecules?

And my usual answer to that is yes, but there are two words I would strike from the sentence, and those two words are "nothing" and "mere". Because matter is not mere; matter is extraordinary, we are made out of matter. The late Carl Sagan characterized us and the place we have in the universe this way: he said that we are a way for the cosmos to know itself. And what the evolutionary process has done is to take the dust of which we are made, the matter and energy of which we are made, and somehow make that matter self-aware. It's an awareness that thrives in each of us in this room and everywhere on this planet. The mystery of how matter becomes reflective and thoughtful and self-aware, from my point of view, is the mystery that biology has always tried to solve. We are closer to solving that mystery today than ever before. Evolution does not explain everything about human nature, but it is the origin of human nature. It's only by understanding our origins that we begin to understand who we are in the first place, and where we might be going. That understanding is, I think, the most precious gift that science can give us.

LANDI: So would you say that we can really understand our origin thanks to the scientific progress?

MILLER: I don't want to say understand in the sense that there's nothing for Rick to do any more in terms of understanding everything completely, because there's always mystery in science. But the markings of evolution are everywhere: in our bodies, in our genetics, in our genome. As I tried to point out, we understand that evolution is the beginning of how we came to be human. It is not the end of it. It is, in a way, our foundation, but it does not limit our potential. When he won the Nobel Prize, William Faulkner famously said that he believed man will ultimately do more than just survive, he will prevail. Ultimately, the biology of our own human nature will be the key to how we will prevail, not just in the struggle for existence, but in the struggle for knowledge and to understand our place in the universe.

LANDI: Martin, what do you think?

NOWAK: Thomas Aquinas said that God is the teacher both in faith and reason, and that's actually the starting point of the *Summa Theologica.* I found that statement very impressive. We like science and we like faith, we like religion, and he asks if both are necessary, and what is the role of each, and if reason alone would be enough. In principle, but it would take too long. Therefore, faith is a kind of shortcut to make it easier for people to understand where they are.

Something else he said is very impressive for me: that every argument against the Christian faith can be shown to be wrong based on reason alone. So if somebody makes an argument against the Christian faith, you do not have to call upon faith; you can actually disprove it by reason alone. Very beautiful. For me, it is obvious that science, mathematics, philosophy—these do not constitute arguments against religion or against Christianity. And the kind of scientific atheism that we are witnessing these days is a kind of a social construct, and is in some sense the formation of another kind of religion. The scientific atheism that is preached by many of my scientific colleagues is almost a new kind of religion, completely overstepping the actual interpretation of the scientific method to say that what we have now learned proves that God doesn't exist, and thereby sort of creating a metaphysical position that in itself is faith-based, like a religion. This shows that humans cannot be without religion, in my opinion. So for me language is a human universal and religion is a human universal. And in the discussion between faith and evolution I want to tell those people of faith to not be afraid of evolution. Evolution is a beautiful scientific theory, and has some explanatory power in the same way that we do not feel challenged by gravity.

You know, if I tell you Newton described gravity in order to explain how the universe looks on a large scale, you don't feel challenged in your Christian faith. Likewise, evolution presents no challenge for the Christian faith. When Newton actually had the mathematical equations for the laws of gravity, for him there was a question, suddenly there was now a challenge.

If I have a mathematical description of gravity, do I take away from God? Newton made the famous remark, "Hypotheses non fingo." I do not make a hypothesis as to why there is gravity, I just describe it mathematically. In the same way, I don't make hypotheses as to why there's evolution, I just describe it mathematically.

LANDI: Yes, exactly. Thank you, because my point was exactly the same. The "why" is a question that doesn't pertain to science per se, science deals more with the "how". But I think that, as you said, the best way to address this question—To what extent can evolution explain human nature?—is by looking at our experience. If we look at our experience, we cannot deny that there is something mysterious about reality. And we, scientists, have this experience all the time: even if we begin with a hypothesis and prove exactly what we predicted, there is a sense of surprise when the results are in front of us. None of us can deny that there is something mysterious that appears all the time. If we look at our experience, I think we have the way to address this question.

I wanted to mention that in his book, *The Religious Sense*, Fr. Luigi Giussani—by the way, Fr. Luigi Giussani, the founder of Communion and Liberation, also wrote a book called *Man as the Self-Awareness of the Cosmos* [*L'autocoscienza del cosmo*]. Exactly what you Ken said, that man is the point of nature in which nature can reflect on itself.

Anyway, in another book, *The Religious Sense*, he wrote, "The modern mentality reduces reason to a group of categories, in which reality is forced to find a place, and whatever does not fall into these categories is defined as irrational. But reason is like an eye staring at reality, greedily taking it in, recording its connections and implications, penetrating reality, moving from one thing to another yet conserving all of them in memory, trying to embrace everything." A human being faces reality using reason. Reason is what makes us human, and it is this broader reason, of which the scientific method is one of the available tools, that governs our experience.

I would like to close, just looking at our experience. If we consider our experience, is it enough for a mother to define her own son as a more advanced, evolved animal? Is this enough for a lover? For a friend? There is something that goes beyond; our experience tells us this.

O'MALLEY
GAGLIOTTI
SHRIVER

Identity and the Challenge of Disability

A dialogue with ***Sean Cardinal O'Malley****, Archbishop of Boston,* ***Timothy Shriver****, Chairman of Special Olympics, and* ***Jean Vanier*** *(on telecast), founder of L'Arche communities, on their discovery of human identity in their life long experiences with people with disabilities. Moderated by* ***Barbara Gagliotti***

Introduction

The condition of people with disabilities cannot be forgotten in any serious reflection on what is our true "I." Rather, it deeply challenges the ideal of self-sufficiency typical of our age and may shed a truer light on the real essence of being human.

BARBARA GAGLIOTTI: Good evening, and welcome to this presentation on Identity and the Challenge of Disability. I am Barbara Gagliotti, an educator and the Associate Director of Crossroads Cultural Center in Washington D.C. I'm very pleased to welcome our guests on behalf of New York Encounter.

His Eminence Cardinal Sean O'Malley, Archbishop of Boston, is a dear friend of New York Encounters. The last time he was on this stage was with our beloved Monsignor Albacete just one year ago, and we had a fitting tribute to Lorenzo last night. To my left is Timothy Shriver. He is an educator, a social activist, an entrepreneur, and he is the head of Special Olympics, an organization which he just told me now numbers more than five million athletes in countries throughout the world. He is [*audience applause*] also the author of the bestselling book Fully Alive: Discovering

Saturday, January 17, 2015

What Matters Most. Congratulations on your book and welcome to New York Encounter.

TIMOTHY SHRIVER: Thank you.

GAGLIOTTI: Our third guest will be joining us via a pre-recorded video interview, and his name is Jean Vanier. Some call him a living saint. He is the founder of the L'Arche communities and network of people living with people with disabilities, and he could not be with us this evening but he did graciously consent to give an interview, an exclusive interview to New York Encounter, which we will see in a second. Our discussion this evening hopes to open the question of human limits and vulnerability, and to challenge somewhat the prevailing image of the self-made man, and self-sufficiency as the paragon of human achievement.

We're now going to watch the interview with Jean Vanier, and I think there is no better person to speak about vulnerability and the resource that it is. When we're finished with that we will come back and have a conversation with our guests.

This year's New York Encounter deals with the issue of identity, the search for the human face. A challenge for all of us, certainly, and, we tend to think, an even greater challenge for people with disabilities, although perhaps they have something to teach us.

Jean Vanier has shared most of his life with people with intellectual disabilities, and has created many communities that provide a place for people to more fully develop their humanity. He has agreed to answer a few questions and to share, with all of you gathered in New York, his experience of the quest for identity in these extraordinary circumstances.

[Video Presentation]

INTERVIEWER: In your opinion, what is the fullness of human life, and how has living with people with disabilities taught you that?

JEAN VANIER: The heart of the center of the human being is the individual conscience. In the Bible they talk about the heart as being the center, but the individual conscience is something very special. It's a capacity of the human being to recognize love and to seek truth, and to seek justice. It's what Mahatma Gandhi would talk about—the little inner voice, the little inner voice. Now, what is the mysterious meaning even to people with severe disabilities? They recognize that they are loved.

You might say that for some people with autism, it's more complex. Yes, let's not get into the realities of that area, some rather more complex realities about communication: How does a man with autism know that he is deeply respected and deeply loved? There is something in the child. The child knows whether he is loved. It's the eyes, it's the smile, it's a whole way of being. It's about the tenderness to approach people tenderly, that is, the quality of touch; and it reveals to people: "You are precious."

We welcomed [Eric] here, and I lived with him for a whole year. Eric was blind, he was deaf, he could not walk, he had very severe disabilities, and he had been in a psychiatric hospital for many years. He had been put in the hospital when he was two; his mother never visited him because she was too shocked. She was living off the shock of having a child like that.

INTERVIEWER: So, what is the role of L'Arche?

VANIER: It's to reveal to Eric: "You are born beautiful." And you dare to believe, because otherwise he's in anguish. Who is he? Nobody wants him, nobody loves him. He has been humiliated. Yes, he's been to doctors and all sorts of good people, but who wants to live so that the whole reality of life is that we live together? We had to learn how to give Eric his bath, holding him in our arms, and communication through body.

And this is somehow the whole story: the Word became flesh. God became flesh to communicate through the body, through touch and through a touch of tenderness. Tenderness is a way of listening without judging, without condemning. See the heart of the mystery of Christianity: be compassionate as my Father is compassion. Do not judge, do not condemn, forgive. So, in some way it's the communication that the other is precious. And it's through this communication that Eric will discover he is someone.

Also, the assistants: they can come, wanting to do good for the people. And they have their diplomas, the good people, they come from the culture, from the culture where it's good to be good, and so on, but being good is not the question. Rather, it's to become a friend. To enter into a relationship, to look into the eyes, to touch people tenderly. People with disabilities teach assistants what it means to be human.

To be human is to live tenderly and kindly. The mystery of people with disabilities is that they are seen as the bottom of humanity, of being no good. So the people who come as assistants, they have to change. They have to change, have to discover that that person with disabilities is precious, and through giving the baths and so on—of course, we have many in L'Arche who are capable and who are doing things, but some also are severely disabled, so a meeting is something special.

And I say that if Jesus calls us to eat together, then to eat together is to have fun. To eat well, to drink well, but to give a meal. Jesus says if you eat with the rejected, those who have been pushed to the periphery, then you shall become blessed. It's not the people with disabilities who will see themselves as blessed—you will become blessed because things will change within you. You will discover that the secret of humanity is that we enter together into the human family and each person is precious. Saint Paul even says that those who are the weakest are necessary to the body, which is the Church.

INTERVIEWER: What hampers or allows the growth of the human person? Is there anything particular about this process for people with disabilities?

VANIER: First of all, it's a long road to grow in love. St. Paul asks, What is love? In the thirteenth chapter of Corinthians, the first letter, he says that love is patient, love is service, love is to believe all, hope all, excuse all. That doesn't come naturally.

To be patient, to have to be in this situation where there is impatience—I mean, we welcomed some years ago Pauline, who had one arm paralyzed, a leg paralyzed, an epileptic, but she was also incredibly violent. And why was she violent? She had lived forty years of humiliation in school, in the streets, in her family, a family that didn't want her in such a condition. To become human is to welcome the other who is different because he or she is a human person. But it takes time because we have to change.

You see, we're in a culture of success and a culture of power, a culture of winning. But it's not a question of being better than you. I'm a person. I'm capable of love. You are too, so we can meet. That is the beauty of the human face. The human face in some way is the revelation through your eyes, through your smile, that you are human. How to grow in that? It's not by reading books. It's not by doing good theology. It's doing what Pope Francis says: go to the periphery, go to the extreme limits, and there become a friend of the poor. And there discover that they will evangelize you, and discover also, if you listen, the wisdom of the poor. That wisdom of the poor could come from those who are in the slum areas of Thailand or wherever. We are in a culture of status, of power; my group, my group is the best group I know. But to be human, it's not a question of me knowing more than you. To be human is to listen to you. That means something has happened inside of me so that I'm able to really be open to the other who is different.

How many people go into the broken areas of New York, just to listen to people? "What is your story? Tell me your story." I remember one of the people of L'Arche worked with prostitutes in Australia, and she told me this story. One day she was in Sydney, at the park of Sydney, and she met a young man whom she had followed a bit, accompanied, and he was dying of an overdose. He said to her, just the last words, "You've always wanted to change me. You have never met me." Meet a man who's been caught up in prostitution and say, "Tell me your story." You'll find that he has had a story of pain, rejected by his parents, in a gang, and all sorts of things; nobody has really listened to his story. That's when we begin weeping together, and we can really start discovering the mystery.

Mother Teresa started welcoming people who were dying. She didn't teach them, she took them in her arms because it is through the body that you reveal that someone is loved. Through a touch, through the eyes, through the face—it's a whole physical reality.

Not to "do something for", but to "be with": it was the touch of Mother Teresa on these people in the streets that revealed to them that they were important. What we discover is that when we are with people who've been seriously rejected and pushed aside, as we enter into relationship with them we are changed. And that is the story.

Which also means, Do we want to change? Do we want to be transformed? Do we want to discover that the only important thing is to love people? Not just to teach them, but to discover their beauty as human beings?

INTERVIEWER: Limits of any types are usually viewed in our society as obstacles to freedom. How does your experience challenge this common belief?

VANIER: Limits. We are all so limited. You know, we were born as tiny babies and people die as very fragile people. The history of each one of us is to grow from littleness, to gradually discover who we are and what it means to be a human being. Then we start going downhill. I'm eighty-six now, but come and see me in five years' time: I probably won't be speaking. To be limited is to be human. To be unlimited is to be God. The danger is for people to think they're God; but they're crazy if they do. It's that man in the Gospel who said, I'm going to build up my barn and everything, and then God says, You're nuts! You're going to die. Tonight we can develop a cancer that springs forth. What does it mean to be human? It's to love, and to love we need to be loved. We need to live a relationship, to live a relationship, and we all know that if a child has been abused as a child, and violated sexually or physically, we know that that child will be in danger of not being able to grow humanly until maybe the day of their death. Maybe the day of their death they will discover something.

To be limited is to be human. To be vulnerable is to be human. Because any of us this night can have a diagnosis of cancer or something, and all of us know that at a particular moment we will die. That is the story of what it means to be a human being, to go from a sentiment of being able to do things, to the deep understanding that we're all broken, we need help, we need to be loved. As we fall into the period of sickness we need help, we need love; we need kind, competent doctors, we need good nurses, we need a loving family, we need a community, we need to be together. The problem of humanity today is an extreme individualism. We've lost the sense of community, and community is not just a group of people living together in a cloister. Community is about coming together for a mission. The community of L'Arche has a mission: to reveal to people, however deep their disabilities, that they are precious; and then to discover that as we do that, I—we—are changed.

So for that person I spoke about in Australia, to listen to that man who was involved in prostitution, you need a community. If you're all alone, you're not going. We all need to be together, to give support to each other, to love each other, to tell each other we have a place in the body of Christ. St. Paul says that those who are the weakest are absolutely necessary to the body of Christ. Because when we're weak we say, "I need your help."

And it's when we say, "I need your help, I cannot do it alone," that we become human. When we think we're God, when we think we have all the power, when we think we have all the knowledge and everything, then no. Humanity has to become weak to discover its gifts, then also to discover, "I need your help." [*audience applause*]

GAGLIOTTI: Just a quick word of thanks to Paolo Silvano, who helped us with that interview in France.

Your Eminence, we heard Jean Vanier speak of the wisdom of the poor. You have spent a considerable amount of time living and working among the poor in Washington D.C., in the Virgin Islands, and now in Boston. I just read a month ago that the poverty level is at its highest in Massachusetts since the 1960s. Can you share with us some of the wisdom of the poor?

CARDINAL SEAN O' MALLEY: Well, thank you very much. First of all, I want to say how pleased I am to be here today. Last year I was on the stage with Monsignor Lorenzo Albacete, and I never imagined that it would be the last time we would be here together. But it's an honor to be back. I know that with this Encounter you're honoring his legacy and his memory, and I'm happy to be back to be a part of that. [audience applause] It is very moving to listen to the testimony of Jean Vanier; it's the second time that I've seen this interview. He certainly is a man whose faith has transformed him, and allowed him to have a vision of humanity and our connectedness with God and with one another. He is just such a gift to the Church and to the world. I'm also very honored to be with Tim Shriver, who is, like Father Vanier, so involved in work with the disabled. I was privileged to know Tim's parents. I met him when he was thirteen years old because we invaded his house with scores of farm workers who amassed there with Cesar Chavez, and he remembers the confusion.

But the poor have very much to teach us; there's no doubt about that. When I was the bishop of Fall River, we took on a parish in Honduras, a very poor rural parish. Every year we would send down groups of students from the university, along with the chaplain, to work in the parish. When they would come back I would always meet with them and say, Well, what did you think of your experience in Guaimaca? And they would say, Oh bishop, we never saw such poverty, I mean you know, people living in those shacks, dirt floors, no running water, no schools, working so hard in the fields and no cars or television sets—and they're so happy! I mean this was what amazed the young people from Massachusetts in this Third World experience.

Anyone who has the privilege of working very close to the poor sees how often their sense of values is so very different from the sort of bourgeois way we look upon things in the United States. First of all, during twenty years in Washington working with immigrants from Central America, I was always so truly struck by how these people come to America, work so hard, and some of them send half of their earnings back to relatives in their country to support them. In many countries of Central America the largest part of the gross national product is the money sent back by these immigrant families working minimum wage jobs or less, and in those same homes you see that there is always be room for someone else. If a child's parents died, there was always a family who would take them in. They were welcome to stay in their apartment and share the little food and resources that they had. There is an openness to life and a generosity, and a primacy given to relationships when people are not surfeited with material things. I think there's a very strong witness in that for in our lives.

GAGLIOTTI: Tim, your mother was Eunice Kennedy Shriver. She was the sister of President John Fitzgerald Kennedy and Senators Robert and Ted Kennedy, and she was the driving force behind the Special Olympics. As early as the 1960s she opened your house to people with disabilities and Camp Shriver. Can you tell us a little bit about that? What motivated her to do that kind of work?

SHRIVER: I think the simple answer to that is her own sister. But before I talk about her sister, my Aunt Rosemary, I also would like to acknowledge your Eminence, and of course, Jean Vanier, who is a personal hero to me and to my wife Linda and to our children. We visited him in his community on four or five different occasions, really a—"living saint" is of course sometimes overused, though I'm sure there are many living saints even in this room—but his witness to the importance of a relationship, to the practice of unconditional love, to the patient exercise of community and compassion, is quite extraordinary.

Normally when I give a talk there's about thirty or forty people in the room, so if you don't mind, your Eminence, I'd like to have you come with me in the future! [*audience laughter*] I think I'll sell a lot more books. Probably not realistic, but it's a nice idea anyway. All the proceeds from the book go to Special Olympics, so you don't have to worry about conflicts.

Anyway, in trying to capture in my own way my own experience with people with intellectual differences over the course in my own life, twenty years, our marriage, the raising of children, I kept finding myself being told, Oh, that's so nice that you do that work. It's so wonderful that you're such a good man, so kind! Isn't it wonderful the way you help them?

And those kinds of comments revealed to me that many people misunderstood the revolutionary nature of the work, the transformative nature of the engagement of the connection of the relationship, even the distinction between them and us, between those with disabilities and those of us who do not have disabilities.

How many people in this room don't have vulnerabilities or weaknesses? How many people would be proud to have those [vulnerabilities] be your label, by which you were introduced to everyone in the world, the one most vulnerable part? If you let me label you that, and put it on your birth certificate: this is who you are—a person with this vulnerability—let me put it on your school forms, let me put it everywhere you go. It is in some ways violence that we do in separating ourselves from one another with these terms, even though we use them for convenience and often with good intention.

Our own scriptural tradition begins with a very important dimension of creation, which is that in the beginning God creates, and God sees what He has created. God does not distinguish between the good things He created and the not so good things. The strong things and the weak things, the beautiful things and the ugly things, the rich things and the poor things. No, God looks on all the things He has created and says they're good. Later on we find Adam and Eve cowering in fear. Later on we find someone saying I'm afraid, I'm naked, but God doesn't say that. God doesn't tell us to be afraid of being naked. God doesn't tell us that we're disabled, old, fat, poor, weak, vulnerable. This is a long history we're trying to overcome: healing our sense that those who have some form of difference are in some way different from the rest of us; that there is even a "them" and an "us" when there is really only an "us".

In my view, if there's one lesson of religious life, of religious practice, it is that there is only "us", there is no "them". In my mother's family—sorry for the long introduction Barbara—but in my mother's family were nine children raised in Boston to an Irish Catholic family filled with faith, filled with devotions, in the traditional Irish sense, daily attendance at Mass, devotions to the Saints, praying the Rosary, all these kinds of things—but also a tremendously competitive, ambitious group of human beings. [*audience laughter*] I just have to think that, at some level, the high end of the Holy Spirit works here, because into that very competitive environment comes someone who, so to speak, cannot keep up. My mother would say, "You know, my father would ask us all at the dinner table, 'What did you think of today?' And we'd go around and Joe and Kathleen and Jack would answer in unison, and Rosemary, of course Rosemary couldn't answer the way her brothers and sisters could, and she would be skipped over.

They would look for the Church to come through with some kind of explanation, or our school, and the Church was responsive; but there was nothing for Rosemary. My mother would say this almost like a victim of post-traumatic stress. Even into her eighties, she would remember her mother picking up the phone and then putting it down, saying, You know, there's nothing for Rosemary, nothing.

Nothing, nothing. A culture so full of values, yet it devalues someone who speaks more slowly, who learns differently, who doesn't run as fast or work as quickly or perform as brilliantly. They kept her at home and said, Rosemary's your sister, you include her. Rosemary's your sister, you include her. To be honest, I have to think that the—you know, Barbara mentions, of course, President Kennedy and Senators Robert and Ted Kennedy, and these are very prominent members of my family. But almost no one knows the leaven in their lives, the ways in which they learned—to the extent they did—that the art of politics is the art of extending the boundaries of inclusion. The art of politics is breaking down boundaries of hate and fear based on race, based on poverty, based on disability, the things that they're known for, President Kennedy in particular. Asking people to give of themselves to others.

"Ask not what your country can do for you, ask what you can do for your country." Where did he learn it? Where did he learn to have the confidence to say to two hundred million people, I need your help?

I don't think he learned it from studying the British politicians, I don't think he learned it from Lincoln, or from his own experience in the war. I think he learned it from Rosemary. I think he learned from the faith that taught him to include Rosemary, and the sure sense that when he included her, when he welcomed her, when he sailed with her, he got something quite beautiful in return: the sense that he was loved unconditionally. I have to believe that as wonderful as my grandparents were, they drove their children; and as children often do, they probably confused how hard they had to work with how lovable they were, how much they had to perform with how good they were. Rosemary would not have evaluated her sisters, or she certainly didn't evaluate me when I came home from school with a C-plus on a test. It didn't matter to her. If I had just missed the cut on the varsity team, it didn't matter to Rosemary. I could sit with her and play cards and sit at dinner, and now we both would sit there and be so excited, the dessert was about to come—it didn't matter. There was a sense in which we were one.

GAGLIOTTI: Let's see if we can go a little bit deeper into this question of vulnerability and limitedness that both of you have spoken about, and certainly Jean Vanier spoke about it in the interview. What have you learned about your own identity in dealing with situations of vulnerability or your own vulnerability?

SHRIVER: She's looking right at me. [*audience laughter*]

GAGLIOTTI: I'm gonna ask the Cardinal. We'll come back to you.

SHRIVER: I just want to make sure that the Cardinal isn't—I mean, I've just spoken for a long time, so I'm scared up here, what can I tell ya? [*audience laughter*]

O' MALLEY: Well, I have more vulnerabilities. When I was young and in school I was—probably because in my family there wasn't anyone with Down Syndrome—I was sort of afraid, and I didn't know how to react when you would meet someone with Down Syndrome. We had some very good friends who were active in the Catholic Worker movement, and they took me to visit a family, the Gauchat family, Bill and Dorothy Gauchat, who were very good friends of Dorothy Day. They had six children, and they started the Catholic Worker movement in Cleveland. They had a farm at Avon, Ohio, and on their farm they had a large house where they took in children whose parents were unable to cope with the disabilities that they had.

Many of them were very severely deformed, with very severe brain damage, and it was kind of shocking to me when I first saw all these children. But then, after being with this family for a couple of hours, I realized these children were like a love bomb that had landed in the middle of their family. They had learned to love in such a special way because of these children. These children were teaching them their own humanity, how to relate; and it was a transformative moment in my life.

I was privileged to be with the Holy Father last year when he went to Assisi. Pope Francis, who speaks and gestures all the time, it's just amazing—the first place he wanted to visit was the Istituto Serafico, which is a hospital for children with Down Syndrome and other kinds of physical and mental ailments. The Holy Father wanted his pilgrimage in Assisi to begin there. Afterwards I thought, You know, it's so appropriate, because Saint Francis's conversion, as he describes in his last testament, takes place as a young man when he is confronted by someone with leprosy. Saint Francis had this almost terrible phobia, and whenever he would see a leper he would just run in the other direction. But this particular day the grace of God touched his heart and he got off his horse, went over to the leper, kissed him, gave him all of his money, gave him his clothes; and later, before he died, when he's writing about his life, he said that was the moment. That was the moment: everything that before had seemed bitterness was now changed into sweetness.

SHRIVER: Yeah, so beautiful.

O' MALLEY: That was his conversion. And so for the Holy Father to choose the Istituto Serafico as the beginning of his visit to Assisi... He read a letter there he had received, I think, when he was Archbishop in Buenos Aires, a letter which I've written a little quote from right here. It says, "Dear Francis, I am Nicholas. I am sixteen. I cannot write to you directly because I don't speak and I don't walk. I've asked my parents to write this letter. I received my first communion when I was six and now I'm preparing for confirmation, something that makes me very, very happy. Every night since you asked for it, I pray to my guardian angel who is called Eusibius, and who is very patient." [*audience laughter*]

The Holy Father went on to talk about the children there. He said, These children are like the wounds on Christ's body. When the Resurrected Lord came back, you know, all of the wounds were—I mean, so much of it was healed, but the wounds of the nails were still there and He showed those as a sign of His love. The Holy Father said: after all of these Easter apparitions where the Risen Lord shows these wounds, He takes those wounds up to heaven. He said, These children are like those wounds, and when we're in contact with him, we're in contact with Christ's wounds in heaven.

As people of faith, I think we have to see each other differently; as Jean Vanier, living at L'Arche, has told us. It will change everything that is bitter into sweetness.

SHRIVER: I came to the Special Olympics movement thinking I was coming to help. So much of what gets confusing in religion is that morality and ethics tend to be perceived as exhortations, as duties, obligations, things you're supposed to do; you ought to be a good boy or a good girl, you ought to help the poor, you ought to give money.

All of a sudden I discovered—and I won't go through the whole story because it's a long one—that that was all wrong. That there was no "ought" in the Gospel. Here's how I discovered it. After some time watching people with intellectual challenges and differences, I'll invite you to participate in this exercise a little bit. Imagine that behind me is a track, you're sitting in bleachers, it's a nice warm day, you've got your coffee or your newspaper, and you're watching a race. You've chanced upon a high school track, and there's a Special Olympics event going on. There are parents scattered about the stands and you're there together with them.

And then you look down towards the starting line and you see six or eight youngsters lined up, maybe twelve, fourteen years old, and they're getting ready to run their race.

You pause and maybe have a moment of self-awareness in which you recognize that maybe the 12-year-old who catches your eye down on that track, who has Down Syndrome, you know that when she was born and her mom or dad said, Doctor, is the baby okay? that the doctor probably said, We're not sure.

And you know that when that little girl was trying to walk it took her longer, and all the other moms were saying, You know, my baby is walking, at ten months or twelve months, but maybe this little girl didn't walk until eighteen or twenty months; and you know that when you looked for child care most of the child care centers said, No, I'm sorry, we don't have a program. And you know that the school said the same thing—maybe a special program, maybe not.

You know that she grew up, as one parent told me, never being invited to the birthday parties. She's down on that track now, and you can imagine that she's trained for her moment to run her race. She gets in her lane and the starting gun goes off. Down the track she runs behind me, keeping her arms striding in going through to the finish line as she's been taught by her coach—and she comes in third. She turns up into the stands near you and you can hear her mother screaming Yaaay! Congratulations! And her arms go up in the air: third place!

After a while, I start to see that I want to be like her. I want to be that unafraid, to do my best. I want to be able to come in third if that's as fast as I can run and still have my mother cheer for me. I want to be able to put my arms up and be unafraid of what anybody thinks, that this is who I am.

This is my race. I just won it. And if you don't think I'm a winner, then you don't understand winning. If you think I came in third, and that's not as good as second, then you don't understand what it means to do your best. You don't understand excellence, you don't understand dignity, you don't understand love, you don't understand joy, you don't understand anything—and that was me. I really don't think I understood any of those things.

Until I finally took seriously that she won a medal. You know, sometimes people say to me, Tim, do you go to the real Olympics? Boston's bidding for the real Olympics right? [*audience laughter*] And I always just say no. We have a good, you know, sort of a bureaucratic answer. But after a while I had to stop and think: Do I go to the real Olympics?

You bet I do. You bet I do. [*audience laughter*]

If I take seriously, you know, that the medal she won, that you just watched her win, is a real Olympic medal, then I have to change everything. If it's just a symbol, if it's just a symbol of goodness or greatness, then I'm a liar. If

I really think she's just as gifted, beautiful, strong, and wise as anybody else in this room, as anybody else I've ever met, as any Nobel laureate, as any politician or CEO, then I have to change everything. In this way I think of Flannery O'Connor, whose own reflections on the Blessed Sacrament, you know—at one point I think someone outside said to her, Well, don't you think it's just a symbol? And I think her response was, If it's just a symbol, then to hell with it.

Because it's a lie. But if it's real, then that's something to believe in. It'd be something to transform and change your life. I love when Pope Francis invited the Church to see itself as a field hospital, because I spent a lot of time on fields. We are, in some respects, a sacramental kind of presence. A presence of opposites, a presence of contrast, a presence of the divine, infused into the human. A presence of complete humanity and yet complete sacredness at the same time, because we do bring those who are seen as losers.

I mean, let's be honest: the reason we're talking about disability is because we're afraid of it. The reason we're here trying to figure out what to do about it is because we don't understand our limitations, as Jean Vanier said. We are afraid of our weakness and our vulnerability. That twelve-year-old represents to most of us all the things we're most afraid of. Not being smart in the traditional sense, not being rich in the traditional sense, not being independent in the traditional sense, not being popular in the traditional sense, not having a good business card, not having a good bank account, all those things; that's what she represents.

Whether we like it or not, it's true. And until we face it and convert it into a strength that Paul talks about in his letter to the Corinthians, where the wise are shamed by the weak; until we recognize it as an invitation to discover ourselves—not to do our duty, but to discover our true selves, if you will, as your fellow Franciscan, your Eminence, Richard Rohr, sometimes writes about; until we invite ourselves into that experience of relationship without which we fear, we will always exclude, we will always say some things are good and some things are not, unlike God. To the extent we're all trying to get back to God, we have to confront all the things that we're afraid of, because they're all made by God and they're all where we're headed, in my view.

GAGLIOTTI: Okay, you're leading to the next question I was going ask, because what you're saying is something radical. Both of you are suggesting something radical that we are afraid of, but how can we see our vulnerability and our limitedness as resources for us personally, but also for the world?

O' MALLEY: I think one of the biggest deficiencies of our modern culture is the extreme individualism. I know Professor Putnam has that great book, Bowling Alone, where he documents how each generation of Americans is becoming more isolated, more alone, more individualistic, joining less with others, with people living alone and eating alone. The whole phenomenon of the autonomous self, where individuals become so absorbed in themselves that they really lose touch with others.

To really understand our humanity is to understand our interdependence. Jean Vanier alluded to this when he said, No matter how strong and healthy anyone is, there are periods in your life when you are completely dependent on the goodwill and love of other human beings. Particularly for the first years of your life, and very probably for the last years of your life. This interdependence is what makes us human: we're not autonomous selves, we are connected to each other. Our own limitations are a way of sharing in that common humanity and feeling responsible for one another. And I think that's a very important lesson to be learned in any kind reflection around these issues.

SHRIVER: I don't think we have to glamorize vulnerability beyond its presence in all of our lives; it is usually pretty close to the surface. We're afraid of it. I don't think we have to glamorize it. I think the reason why so much of our tradition and so much of our experience is afraid of it is because it exposes us to one another. It exposes us in some respects as being like the other. It doesn't allow us to build a wall, we're not better than the other. At the end of the day, no one's better than another. I'm sorry to say it, but it's true. We spend a lot of time trying to be better than others. Churches do this, political institutions do this, businesses do this; we try to make someone have the appearance of being better than someone else. It's not true. It's a lie. No one's better than another, and vulnerability reminds us of that at some level. I think you can also see this a lot in the contemplatives. Saint Francis's conversion is a great reminder that sweetness came from realizing he could get off his horse and no longer be afraid of the vulnerability of the disease. The disease was the demon there, right?

The disease, the fear of the disease, the fear of the person; I can't touch that. And so in contemplative experience, and I believe in authentic service experiences as well, reciprocal experiences, we come to vulnerability as a key. We don't have to spend too much time glamorizing it, but it is a key to our common humanity. It is the inescapable link that we share, right? We maybe have many other things that are different, but that, in moments of silence, and in moments of connection, reminds us of our ultimate destiny. I mean, why else do people—again, I'll use my own experience in this: it looks so simple, we run track meets, soccer games, basketball games, what's the big deal, you know? There's nothing theological about it, there's nothing political about it, we don't march on City Hall, we don't throw rocks at organizations that are discriminatory, we just play basketball.

I'll tell one story in the book. I'll tell it very quickly, of a little boy, Donald Page, who was born in a small village in Ireland, and develops a very serious disease, almost dies three or four times. But his mom and dad—his dad's a dairy farmer, eight children—they raise 'em. Ends up in a small school, special needs kids with very, very, significant disabilities. And when the Special Olympics World Games are held in Dublin, they arrange to have a demonstration of people, what we call motor activities people, that have such significant limitations that they can't compete in traditional sports, but can do individual activities.

So his dad told me that Donald was put on the bus in the morning to ride to Dublin for the day, while his mom and dad left in separate cars because they wanted Donald to be with his team. Long story short, I end up being invited to go with this particular van. Linda and I and our kids were there the whole week, but I got a call that morning from the President of Ireland's office saying the president would like to come and go to one of the events, would I accompany her? Of course, I'm so thrilled and flattered, and would she like to go to the motor activities? I'm thinking to myself:

You know, we have athletes who are swimming in Olympic times, we have athletes running marathons, I wish I could take her somewhere she can see these people doing extraordinary things, she'd see how gifted they are; instead, she wants to go to motor activities. I'm thinking, You know, here we sit, right where you guys are sitting, and we get to the hall and it's packed, which is the first shock for me—that people from all over Dublin had come to watch motor activities.

And here comes Donald, wheeled out in his wheelchair to the center of a riser about half this height, and in front of him on a table like this is placed a small bean bag. His job is to perform in front of the president of his country and about fifteen hundred people. To lift the bean bag and move it from one side of the table to the other. His coach stands behind him, and his dad, the dairy farmer, is in the audience. And...go! For about two or three minutes, Donald can't move his arm. The place is quiet. I'm sitting there, uncomfortable like you cannot imagine. And there's Donald, trying to move his arm and it's just not going. He looks around the room, you know, and after about a minute and a half—it's a long time, trust me, to sit there in silence with people, it wasn't contemplative [*audience laughter*], and suddenly his arm starts to move a little bit. At four minutes, a guy in the back yells, "C'mon, lad!" He finally gets his hand onto this beanbag after four minutes.

The crowd starts to cheer. The noise starts to build. His hand moves: eighteen minutes it takes him to lift this bag. The place starts to cheer, and the bag gets higher, and all of a sudden it crosses the midpoint, and the crowd is standing and screaming. I mean you would have thought it was the Final Four and a hundred thousand people, or the finals of the World Cup, Brazil against Argentina, screaming, "C'mon, on lad!" I talk to his dad, who says to me, "I always told the doctors: just give him a bit of time! [*audience laughter*] Donald can do it!"

He puts that thing down and I think to myself—I mean, I'm bawling, the president's sitting next to me, she's bawling, the whole audience is bawling, and I'm thinking to myself: How sad that I was afraid. Lingering in this fear that I had to show off. You know, fifteen years into it, that's why I say I'm a slow learner. I mean it takes a long time.

We all need a bit of time to learn what it means to change our hearts, to convert ourselves, to this possibility that we can redefine human connection, human valuing. I think Donald Page—you know, you think of a country like Ireland and all the things it needs: peace, good political leadership, economic development, and a return to the faith, a stronger church. I firmly believe it needs all of them. But the person most likely to deliver it? Nobel laureate Gerry Adams can do a lot of things, the Church can do many things, but Donald can do things none of them can do in terms of helping that country find its heart.

I think we have to remember that these are invitations, these exhortations to awaken ourselves to the beauty of the human face. Let's not forget that this culture's at war with the human body. Walk up and down the streets here, you'll be told the thousands of things you can do to fix your face, to change it, to color it, to tighten it, to operate on it—and to do the same to the rest of your body, too. We are not comfortable in this culture with the human face. How many people stand in front of the mirror and really, deeply believe that what they're looking at is beautiful? Might say it, but really deeply believe it? Don't you look and think to yourself, If only this were...[*audience laughter*], if only this was...[*Shriver pulls and pushes face, audience laughs*], it would look so much better. I don't think Donald does that.

GAGLIOTTI: One last question. We heard Jean Vanier speak about the need to be friends with people who are more vulnerable than we are, and I want to ask about your experience of friendship. I have particularly in mind Monsignor Albacete, who was not afraid to be vulnerable. Can you tell us about your experience of friendship with him?

O'MALLEY: Well, friendship is what makes us fully alive, to use the name of Tim's book. Not to have friendship is the greatest impoverishment. But I'm thinking about one of my parishioners in Washington who had five children. One of her daughters had Down Syndrome and died when she was thirty-five. I officiated the funeral.

After the funeral, the mother said, "No, Padre, I really need to talk to you." I sat down with her and she said, "When this daughter was born, I was so angry at God, I asked why this happened to my family." And then she said, "This little girl grew up and taught us all how to love. And my husband died, and my children got married, moved away, and this was the daughter that stayed home with me and she was my best friend, and now I've lost her."

But being friends is what brings joy to our life and our existence, and is really what makes us human. Our friendships with people who have Down Syndrome or other limitations make us human. I'm glad that Tim mentioned how our culture has been so caught up in it's own ideal, the cult of physical beauty, or youth, which really warps our minds. Galdos, the Spanish author, has a book called Marianela, and in the book there's this young woman who has a great capacity for friendship and love and goodness and she has a boyfriend, Pablo, who is blind. Marianela cooks for Pablo, she washes his clothes, she goes on walks with him, and is his constant companion. Then Pablo's family sends him off to the big cities where, operated on and cured of his blindness, he comes home.

For the first time in his life he sees this woman who loves him more than anyone else in the world. But now that he can see, he realizes there are other young ladies prettier than Marianela in the village, and he goes and marries someone else. I mean the irony is, when he was blind, he could see the goodness, the love, and the beauty. But when he can see with his eyes, he could only see what was on the surface.

This is what our culture is instilling in people. I mean, the eating disorders that exist today are a result of people being burdened with this idea that beauty means you have to look like, you know, Twiggy or something. And so helping us to discover what real beauty is about, and helping others to discover the beauty that is in them, is important. The Holy Father has said that even when we want to teach the faith, we have to begin with the via pulchritudinis, the way of beauty. That beauty is a reflection of God's eternal beauty, and certainly in friendship it's one of the most beautiful forms of God's beauty that we have.

GAGLIOTTI: Thank you, thank you both. We could probably stay here all day and listen to the stories. This is beautiful. But we don't have the time, so I'd like to thank everyone for being here.

HOLTZ
MEDINA
BURRIS

How Can Education Bring Out Our Identity?

A discussion with ***Darren Burris,*** *Director of Instruction, Boston Collegiate Chartered Schools, and* ***Fr. Albert Holtz, OSB,*** *teacher, St. Benedict Prep., Newark, moderated by* ***Fr. José Medina,*** *U.S. Coordinator of Communion and Liberation, on the future of education in the U.S.*

Introduction

Not long ago, the two institutions that most shaped our identity were the family in which we were born and the schools we attended. Today, the education system seems to have given up on the formation of human identity. Curricula seem to be increasingly focused on "doing" more than "being." Religious and cultural differences find less and less space in schools where a nominal commitment to diversity often translates into the refusal to acknowledge any tradition. The recent discussions about the Core Curriculum have also brought to the fore some important questions about the role of education in forming our national and individual identity. How can the schools help shape the identity of the young, respecting both their freedom and what they have received from their families and their communities? How can educators foster a complete human formation, and not just transmit purely instrumental knowledge and skills? How can a young person today be helped discover his or her true identity? These and other questions will be discussed by a panel of experienced educators.

JOSÉ MEDINA: Good afternoon, everybody. I'm very happy to have with me two people we co-opted without lying, to come and talk to us and resolve the problem of education in the world. I found

Saturday, January 17, 2015

the two brightest people in the world and they're gonna answer all the questions correctly and finally we can put this to bed. [*audience laughter*]

They are Father Holtz—he works at Benedictine Prep, and is one of the founding Benedictine monks of a very successful urban school in Newark.

And Darren Burris, who works in our charter school, a very successful one in Boston. The name is Boston Collegiate. Our intention today is to have a conversation around the aspects of identity. When we think about education, when we think about the question of education, we, all of us, have very high expectations. We not only want our children to be well-educated, we want to also solve the problems of our society. Think about the impact of, or the intention of, *Brown vs. Board of Education*. We want it to be of high quality, we want to actually help the students to become themselves, better persons, we want almost everything and we expect everything from it.

Yet when we start talking about it we have a hard time trying to wrap our head around it. The intention of today is to look at how two educators who have been in the field for many years respond to some of those questions.

I actually asked them to do this in the form of a dialogue, in the form of asking each other questions. Yes, to make it a little bit more lively, we will not allow you to ask any questions. You can do so to them afterwards. I want to begin, yes, very briefly asking both of them to give us a sense of how they work around one very simple question. When we think about identity in schooling, at the school level we think about the mission of the school. We try to understand what it is we are trying to do.

Successful schools nowadays are very purposeful with regards to what they are trying to do. They think about what to use, aware of what the culture of the school is, and that culture has an origin, has the origin of a group of educators who get together and think about it, and work together. It's not that we were born learned; basically we experiment with your children. That's what teachers do, we experiment with your children. [*audience laughter*]

So, Father Holtz, if you can tell us a little bit about where you work, and what makes that place special in your eyes?

ALBERT HOLTZ: Okay. I've only been given a certain number of minutes, so don't worry, I can't go on as long as I'd like. Saint Benedict's Prep was founded in 1868 on the outskirts of Newark, which is now in the middle of downtown. And because of all the social unrest and the Newark riots in '67 and so on, our white prep school that was then a hundred years old closed. But there were a bunch of young Benedictine monks in the monastery at the time who said, Well, we have a vow of stability, we're not going anywhere, what can we do? So we were dumb enough to reopen the school, but this time for majority black and latino kids. And none of us knew what we were doing. We had no money, but we had buildings and a faculty.

So what I'd like to do is share with you what we've been doing for the past 42 years. Specifically eight different facets, from which I've only chosen eight. Here are some programs that are the hidden curriculum. Yes, we teach all the subjects—we're a college prep school, we get kids into Bates and Brown and New Penn and Yale; but for me, what I want to share with you are the things we do. Five hundred and fifty boys. All boys. I guess it's three-quarters—no, two-thirds are African-American. Another large group are Hispanics, most of them from the City of Newark and East Orange in Irvington, socio-economically all the same.

Our school is family-style. Each student belongs to one of eighteen homeroom groups, but the groups are—well, the reason I say "family-style" is that each group is made up of kids from the 7th through the 12th grade. So we've got big brothers built-in to the situation. Also it's cross-age tutoring, and even cross-age counseling. A kid can identify with the group, and each group is named after a famous person in the history of Saint Benedict's Prep, going back many years. Every day we get together as a school, everybody. We take attendance and so on, so it's one big homeroom. Again, the kid gets a sense of belonging to a much larger entity where we read Scripture, we sing, then we take attendance, make announcements.

But the fascinating part is that it's all run by the students. That's the next big thing for us. A crucial principle at our school is: never do anything for a student that he can do for himself. And the amount of money that we spend on people in schools doing stuff that a 17-year-old can easily do is a shame, right? Like taking attendance. The kids know who they are better than...[*audience laughter*]

So for 42 years the kids have been taking the official attendance. Our students take leadership roles in things like running that morning convocation the other day. Five hundred and fifty kids sitting in there, and one of the seniors was fed up because too many kids were talking while someone was making an announcement. He stood up and dressed them down, and told them to shut up, and then everybody was, "Yeah, you're right." That's the way the school runs. The adults—you don't need the adults there for that part.

Membership is not handed to you. Again, we are a monastery school, so when you walk in, you get a grey hoodie, and that's yours for the year, for one year. If you come through with the three As—academics, activities, and attitude—then you can get your black hoodie, which looks remarkably like a Benedictine habit with its capuche. But you might not get it; you've got to earn it. It's something that you do earn. On our ship, there are no passengers, no can-I-just-pay-my-tuition blah blah blah stuff. Nobody pays what it costs. But on our ship, when you get on board we hand you an oar, so you're crew, no passengers. And that's something that I think is very important for kids to identify themselves with. A new freshmen comes in and spends a week in school sleeping on the gym floor at night, in a program run by sophomores and juniors, again because kids run the school. And he learns all about the school. And he also learns that he can do things he didn't think he could do as far as overcoming difficulties and pressures.

It also breaks down the problem of the fear that's bred by ignorance. We have black kids, white kids, we got Buddhists and all sorts of people, all mixed together, and that's an important part of who we are. The freshman year ends with the 53-mile backpacking hike on the Appalachian Trail, from High Point down to the Delaware Water Gap. These are kids from the city. They have to hike 53 miles with a backpack. There's an honor code, and no locks on lockers. Again, because we know you're capable of being honest and we expect you to be honest. We have a huge counseling department much bigger than...I don't know of any high school that comes even close, because we realize that some kids are dealing with so much stuff at home that we cannot expect them to do geometry unless we give them a lot of help.

We have groups that meet as often as they need to: Alateen, kids with no fathers, anger management, a couple of others like that, it's just a part of school life.

In conclusion, I say this is the hidden curriculum of our school. I could show you the course of studies—it looks like that of any other school—but the hidden curriculum that helps the kids to discover their human face is what I thought would be a fascinating thing to give to this discussion. We've been doing it for 41 years now, and it works.

MEDINA: Father Holtz, you call it the hidden curriculum because you expect the kids to learn something out of all of those activities. What are they learning out of those activities?

HOLTZ: Well, I think that's why it fits so nicely with our topic today. They learn that they're lovable, and capable. "I'm capable." So when somebody says to me, I want you to run this group, I want you to stand up and run this meeting of 550 kids...Me? Yeah, you can do that, I'm sure you can do that. I'm capable of carrying a 30-pound backpack 53 miles in this place that's filled with bears and snakes and man-eating God-knows-what, because the seniors tell the freshmen, "You goin' on the trail, man? Oh, man, you gotta be careful, there's monsters in the swamps, they come out of the swamps." [*audience laughter*]

And then of course, "I ain't goin'! I ain't goin'!" What are they learning about themselves, you see? You better be asking that question if you're teaching kids. So if you're teaching a kid and he scores very high on the standardized tests and stuff, but you make them feel like a piece a crap in the process, as a Christian that's not satisfactory for me. Frankly, when he dies the Lord's not going to ask him what his scores were. He's going to say, "Who did you love?" Right? And "How did you love?" The hidden curriculum, then, is just simply all those things that make this student feel the way he feels.

Watching the interaction of the faculty, that's hidden curriculum. We don't encourage experimentation around here, we don't encourage people being a little bit out of the ordinary, we don't encourage people to be...well, that's hidden curriculum. So we try to be real careful about that, and sometimes very explicit about that.

When we want silence in that room of 550, the hand goes up and the kids theoretically get quiet. And if they don't get quiet fast enough, we gotta come back after school and practice. We never punish, never punish. We might practice until 5:30 in the evening, but we don't punish. [*audience laughter*] We just practice.

MEDINA: Darren Burris is the best math teacher that I know. Math is famously the most hated subject. I wanted to hear from you, Darren, on how you see this hidden curriculum interacting with math.

DARREN BURRIS: Sometimes in mathematics there's sort of a cultural baggage. Whether students like it or not, at times they feel worse about themselves if they can't do it. They make excuses for not being able to do it. When you're a math teacher, there's this extra kind of need to deeply reach all students, because the students who don't learn math actually feel worse about themselves.

When you're thinking about the hidden curriculum and reaching all learners, it needs to be about what they know and where they can go. About growth as opposed to meeting one particular mark this day, by creating opportunities for them to meet it over time. It's about teaching them that they can solve problems, even if that one particular math concept is elusive. You're teaching them to be a problem solver. You're teaching them to be a collaborative thinker. You know, you wanna put tests in front of them that require them to rely on others. Sometimes math instructions are so very individualized—as opposed to teaching them about what it means to work with others to solve a problem.

I think also there's a little bit of a sense that kids tie their own success to that long term as well, so it's also about painting math as something that's for them no matter what they are. Whether it's as simple as getting them to buy into investments, or understanding the world, understanding the events around them, by making it engaging enough and relevant enough for them that they find it's something meaningful. You kind of move behind the content to just make them understand the world better. That's hard to do.

MEDINA: That is interesting, because in encouraging the person to actually grow in their understanding of self, that identity, the first place the students reach is: What perception does this adult have of me?

So I want to hear about what you have seen, because you also have, as part of your job, the coaching of teachers. How do we adults communicate these expectations, not only verbally, but also in the way in which we do certain things?

BURRIS: In terms of things that are negative, in terms of a student's identity, lots of times teachers—the first thing you want to do is to warn them, you want to warn yourself when you stand up in front of them or interact with students, or with a new teacher: people are given to comparing, talking about which students are better, or, you know, I'm sure all of us have been in classes or been in experiences where it's clear that some are being held up, and some are being held low.

It's very hard, because sometimes the act of praising—at least in the way I was raised, in the classrooms I was in—becomes a comparison. I was never praised for what I did; I was either praised that I did it better than someone else, or I was not praised and seen as not meeting that expectation.

These days, often math instruction is about personalizing, deeply knowing the student, and having them set goals. You set goals for wherever they are in their math continuum, so that that student is thinking about what it is they need to do to get better, not because they want to be better than someone else, or because they're not meeting someone else's expectation, but they are meeting the expectations that you know you have fostered between yourself and them about where they need to go.

But that's very hard. I mean, as a teacher it's hard to look around the room and see 24 different people with 24 different skill sets, life histories and trajectories, and then try to make them find success on their journey. Comparisons can be damning.

MEDINA: Father Holtz, when you were saying to never do for a student what he can do for himself—as adults we tend to have very... I wouldn't say "low expectations," but we are afraid that students will get hurt. We think of our children as very, I mean, "sheltered" in a sense, or that they're gonna get hurt very quickly.

HOLTZ: As idiots. [*audience laughter*]

MEDINA: So when the mother is afraid that her "idiot" children [*audience laughter*] make mistakes, how is that affecting their search for self, their development as human beings?

HOLTZ: Did you ever read that book called *The Nation of Wimps*? It's a marvelous book, *A Nation of Wimps*. It's about the helicopter parents, the helicopter parents at their worst. There's a place for helicoptering your kids, right? I had no idea he was doing it. But hovering over the kids—well, these poor mothers who have to drop their kid off at the front door, and I tell them, "You won't hear from him until you pick him up on Friday," and the tears well up in the mother.

I just said this to a kid on Friday. I said, "Tell your mom I said hello. I talked to her for half an hour after you went through that door over there for your freshmen orientation experience, and she said, 'But he's never been away from me! And then he'll be hiking 53 miles in the woods, with the bears and the jackals and the man-eating boa constrictors!'" [*audience laughter*]

It's not the kids who don't have the confidence, right? It's us. "Oh, oh, kids can never do that." But at Benedictine Prep we do it all the time. We expect kids to be competent: "Load the buses with all the freshmen who are going up onto the Appalachian Trail." You don't think the adults are gonna do that? You got a 17-year-old kid. In other countries, other cultures, right? That kid could be raising a family, 12-year-olds walking around on patrol in the jungles, toting guns—but our kids, you know... So, I think I'm answering your question. [*audience laughter*] Think of something that a 35-year-old man can do that a 17-year-old kid cannot do.

Of course, thank God for things like VCRs. Where's the 6-year old? Here, program the VCR for me. [*audience laughter*] We belong to a consortium of about 25 schools from around the country. We send kids, and one kid was sent from one school to a school down in Houston. He did some volunteer work in the hospital. This was in 1975.

That was when DeBakey was doing his heart research and stuff, and this kid says, Why are you not computerizing this data? In 1974, 1975, everything was on these cards, and he said, This should be on computers. This kid actually started this whole thing in that big hospital, with DeBakey. Yeah, he's a 16-year-old kid, a computer whiz, and says, Why aren't you doing this? He showed them how to do it. That's a true story. All of these children, you know, and Dr. DeBakey didn't know how to do it. I don't know, you gotta trust that they can!

MEDINA: You're in downtown inner-city Newark, which is a very depressed city, yet you're telling us that your children, your kids, your students, are running the school and you're fine with it, which in a sense it sounds like a dream. I mean you gotta really go and see it to believe it. Because just the idea that suddenly everybody is good, it doesn't sound very...

But the question I'm most interested in is: What is it that sustains your belief that actually allowing your kids to risk is not a bad thing?

HOLTZ: It's belief in guardian angels more than anything else, I think. [*audience laughter*] A lot of this is, "Go ahead, give it a shot, see if it works." But seriously, just even as a humanist you would say, I have trust in the basic intelligence of these kids and their basic goodness, and their basic capabilities. The more you raise the expectations, the better the kids are. So we expect that when the hand goes up, you're gonna shut your mouth, and we expect that and we'll keep practicing until the demands are met, because we know you can do it. So expectations are a big part. Our expectations dictate what happens. If we have cops in every hallway, that's telling what the expectations are, right? And we're fortunate, because as a private school we don't have to deal quite so much with that sort of thing, because kids know that we don't have to keep them.

What sustains us in our belief? Well, we've been doing it for 41 years and it works. And, you know, you win a few, you lose a few. You get rained out occasionally but you show up for every game. You just keep going.

Of course, you're going to make mistakes. Mistakes are very valuable. The cognitive research these days is showing that you learn far more from being wrong than you do from getting all the problems right. When you make mistakes, your brain rewires itself. That's what we allow the kids to do: to make mistakes. That comes from our background as Benedictines. Saint Benedict, in his rule for monks, says, Yeah, mistakes are mistakes, but if you hide your mistake and won't admit it, that's when the problems come. That's when you get punished. You don't get punished for mistakes, but if you don't admit your mistake, that's a problem. Can you learn from your mistakes? He knew that in the year 500, and now the cognitive researchers are finding out that you learn more from your mistakes than from your successes.

BURRIS: Can I answer that one, too? That question? I think I'm not as good a humanist and might have a little less faith, but for me, it was that students actually made me believe. I think that I had high expectations because I was idealistic. I entered public education to do something, and thought that I could do something. But I don't know; I'd like to think that I deeply believe that students can meet really high expectations, that any kid can do anything, but I think that for me it was being in a place where people were working hard and then kids actually showing me that they could. And so now it's these stories of kids each year kind of defying their local circumstances and family conditions. Even their sense of self or whatever. I would say that that's what sustains me.

I think it would have been hard if it hadn't worked, if no kid had graduated and gone onto the next thing and been successful. But it's encouraging. When I get a chance to talk to people I can say, Have high expectations; if you're an educator, stick with it, students can do it. But I think I needed a little proof.

HOLTZ: Darren, do you ever lie to your kids, too? That's always—there's no reason why you can't do this homework!

BURRIS: Yeah. [*audience laughter*]

HOLTZ: And you know what? He comes back the next day and says, I got my older sister to help me with it, and here it is, I did it. It's a little lie here and there. If you're a priest you can get away with it. [*audience laughter*]

MEDINA: What is the value of mistakes? Because I mean, with math, as you were saying, the mistakes are ever-present. As a matter of fact, there is no growth without a previous mistake. But in math in particular we are defined, always defined, by the mistakes. As a math teacher, what value do you give to the mistakes?

HOLTZ: I got a D-minus in freshman Algebra. [*to Burris*] You take it.

BURRIS: I would say for me it was, well, at first I thought the mistakes were a reflection upon myself as a teacher. I was teaching in Philadelphia in a large urban high school. When students are out there and they're making mistakes—again, it's that young idealistic self, thinking it was a statement about me. I didn't have any idea that it could have been a process of their learning. I just thought that I'd failed them. I think for a lot of teachers that I work with now, it's about having a plan, knowing that everybody's gonna make mistakes. No matter how great that day was with that student, that student may not understand the concept. You try to find ways to incorporate that.

But once you start doing that, you begin to realize that learning is this negotiation between mistake and growth, a step backward and a step forward. It's not always linear. Sometimes you're gonna need two people to think about something together, you've got to give them wait time, you have to give them time to negotiate, meaning it becomes a lot trickier, a lot lumpier; but once you start bringing the mistakes in then you actually have at your disposal the exact moment that you wanna show them they've learned. When you start moving the mistakes out and they're the bad things, and kids can never seem like they've learned enough, that they've never done a good job—until you start bringing it back to them and say, Let's look at this mistake. You actually capture that moment where you say to them, *You learned.* Like, you've come to something that you didn't know before. But I didn't do that for a long time.

MEDINA: So we send your, our, children to your school. It's a schooling in which everybody can do whatever they want.

HOLTZ: Oh yeah! [*audience laughter*]

MEDINA: What type of place allows for this freedom? What type of structure allows for freedom?

HOLTZ: Family. One time, we were gonna throw a kid out because he was really bad, and...and so we had—we couldn't do that without his student group leader. He's a member of this group of 25 kids, run by this teenager, the senior who was in charge of that group who supposedly knew the kid, and had been dealing with him all year.

And Father Edwin says to this senior in high school, he says, "So, we're gonna throw 'em out. What do you have to say?" And the senior goes, Father Ed, did you ever make a mistake?" Then the kid says, "You know it says in the Holy Rule [*audience laughter*] that you have three." Kid stayed. We didn't throw the kid out. Did you ever make a mistake? Did your spouse ever make a mistake? Did your five-year-old ever make a mistake? What's your attitude towards that?

Teach a kid to play chess. I was in a rather dysfunctional household once as a guest, and the father was playing chess with his seven-or eight-year-old. "That's a stupid move! Why the hell would you do that?" That's dumb. Instead, show him what the problem is with that move. "You see, looking at the rook..." and then the kid goes, "Oh!" There it is. That's what Thomas Aquinas calls the *Illuminatio Vultus*, brother—boing! Oh wow! Let him learn from his mistake instead of berating him for it. So of course, the more mistakes the merrier. A mistake is a mistake when you make it twice. First one's a learning experience. Next time around, wait a minute; now you didn't learn, did ya? Now you're in trouble.

But yeah, I don't want you to think that we—I'm sure you understand, it's not like, "Oh yeah, do whatever you want!" But kids aren't afraid, then, to try stuff, right? In math: "Give this a shot"; "Oh no, I might get it wrong."

MEDINA: So education is about learning to fail?

HOLTZ: No, learning by.

BURRIS: Maybe learning by or learning from.

HOLTZ: Scientists. What do scientists do? Right? What do you do when you're a scientist, as a human being? An old monk once was asked, What do you do in the monastery all the time? "Well, we fall down, and we get up, and we fall down, and we get up again." And we fall down, and we get up. That's life.

So you're gonna tell the kid he's not allowed to fall down? What we do in the school, too, though, is within our cultures: as soon as you walk in the door there is a carved wooden thing that says, "Whatever hurts my brother, hurts me." So when there's somebody failing in the class, part of that is on you, and you, and you, and whatever helps my brother helps me. The competition part for us is pretty much confined to our excellent sports program. You want to compete, go compete against another school.

Our soccer coach has a thing where he says, "Our family versus their team." But we work together. Just the other day I had a kid who didn't get it at all, the thing we're teaching. So I took the brightest kid in the class and I said, "You have 10 minutes to teach this kid all this stuff and it's going to affect your grade." I didn't have to say the second part. I didn't really have to at all. And guess what, right?

When the kid would say to the other, Well, why didn't Father Albert say that? You know? I mean it's simple. But it's my way of teaching it, my approach.

BURRIS: When I think about how to follow that... [*audience* laughter] But here's what I think about freedom in schools: lots of times freedom is this individual kind of right that you have, and when schools think about themselves as places that teach individuals and only them, then you worry about them doing something right. If they're not doing something right, then there are consequences and things like that.

But it sounds like the school that I'm at right now, we're younger and don't have quite as much experience. I think we're trying to become a place like that, but it's a little bit more about figuring out how we can be free together, so that there's mutual accountability. That I can't be just whatever I wanna be. I need to be mindful of those around me, that I'm part of an institution, that we have some shared values or things that we're negotiating together. I think really good schools are places where, when you walk into them, they don't feel like a collection of individuals who are born obeying particular rules. You're disciplining each kid because they each have an infraction, but you're finding ways that they want to be better versions of themselves because of what you've done together. Which sounds like what's going on there. We're trying to get there. But I think that unfettered freedom...that might be, I guess, dangerous. Their communities do things with freedom, and they can do things that are great, and they can also do things that aren't so great. We have these kids coming every day, we've got a hundred of them in this building. *What can we do together?* is the idea, as opposed to, *Does this kid know geometry proof X?* That's just the wrong mentality.

MEDINA: So we asked everybody here about their kids making lots of mistakes, about exposing the kids to reality. When I use this word *reality*, what I mean is, they're gonna go there and they're gonna learn from it by sometimes hitting their head on the wall. We come to realize that maybe these kids can do a lot more, and that we are in a sense robbing them, robbing them of the possibility of actually growing, yes, by protecting them. I'm wondering now what is the role of the adults there in the school? What are we doing there?

BURRIS: Okay, for me, it might sound maybe a little conservative, but I think of the adults as the holders of tradition in the sense that, I myself as a math teacher, I hold the tradition of mathematics. And it's sort of my role to pass that on to the students so they might do with it what they will. I actually have to take that responsibility seriously, because these students will leave me, they will go into the world. Whether they wanna go into college, if they wanna go into a career, or the military, or whatever it is they're going. There are certain things that I need to pass on to them, however that happens. So I feel a very strong sense that, as the adult, I hold the tradition.

The other side of that is that, as the adult, unfortunately, I have to act like—I have to be the one who's willing to always be honest, to always look at myself to make sure that I'm not being biased or whatever, that I can uphold the best expectations in others, that I'm willing to learn from them. I have to embody all of those things that I may actually not be that good at, but being in this place as the adult for these kids actually makes me have to be a better version of myself. Like I have to be the best possible Darren I can be when I'm there.

HOLTZ: Don't ya hate that?

BURRIS: It's terrible [*audience laughter*], it's causing me to sweat. So I have to keep the tradition, but I also have to be the best version of myself.

How Can Education Bring Out Our Identity?

HOLTZ: Maybe it's easier to say what we should not be, too: dispensers of knowledge. Everybody comes in with a little port in the side of their head, and we just dump the knowledge in, you know; that's not our approach, I think. I would hope that now in the 21st century modeling, when you make a mistake, even like losing your temper with the kids, and then you apologize publicly to the kid—"Oh, that's a sign of weakness." No, it's not. Apologizing is a sign of strength, it's modeling. *Control* is an interesting word. Well, if the adults weren't there to control this thing, it would degenerate into chaos.

Last year a group of German educators, Catholic educators, were visiting our school during the morning convocation, and it went rather long. Then the headmaster gets up: we are not going to readjust the schedule, as we sometimes—maybe too often—do; where we'll push the whole thing back ten minutes or something. We're not gonna take time off for spirit or whatever it was; yeah, we're not going to readjust the schedule. And then right after that, the senior group leader gets up, this kid, and he says, "We will readjust the schedule by ten minutes." And everybody says okay; they know who to listen to. You don't need the adult to run the schedule. And the reason this kid did it was because there was a senior U.S. History exam going on, and he knew that they couldn't afford to shorten it up or whatever it was, and very simply: Can you imagine the German educators when they heard this 17-year-old get up and contradict the Director?

And the kids didn't even hesitate. They knew which schedule to follow. "We need the adults to maintain order," you'll hear. That's overblown. If something's getting shaky in our school, like, let's say, stuff in the cafeteria, you know cafeteria's a mess, or something like that—the last person in the world to handle that is going to be a grownup. You bring in the senior group leaders, and: "What the heck's going on in that cafeteria? It looks like a pigsty. You got two days, no, you got one day to fix that. If you don't fix it, then as the adult I'm gonna have to step in." You think they can't fix that? Sure they can. So they don't need us to control it as much as we would like to think.

So modeling is one. I love that thing about reminding them that they're part of a tradition. We stand on the shoulders of Pythagoras and Descartes and Pascal and so on. That's important stuff; we aged, toothless ones are supposed to be doing that, you know. But, I mean, the kid is lovable and capable, he can control himself. And if he gets out of line, you wack him a coupla times. [*audience laughter*]

You know, is this being taped? [*audience laughter*] Because a lot of this stuff I'm talking about is against the law. [*audience laughter*] Like, you're a parent and your kid's not in school. You get a phone call from a 16-year-old. Hi, I'm Larry's group leader. What's the story with Larry? Why isn't he in school? That's illegal, you can't do that. You can't give that information to some other kid and tell 'em to call the parents. But so far we haven't been in jail yet. [*audience laughter and applause*]

MEDINA: If education is about learning these...I'm gonna call them behaviors—or, better than behaviors, this openness to what is in front of me, this wanting to dare and be courageous in front of it and engage with it. Why do I have to learn content? Every kid who is taking a math class in this country, except for the A students, asks, Why do I have to learn math? And usually educators—I was a math teacher at some point—we tend to give the answer of, "Because you're gonna need it in the future." But that's very insufficient. So why is the content important? And when I ask this question to you, Darren, because we've done some common work in the Common Core, there is an intention there that is intriguing to me, in trying to understand why content is important for ultimately deciding these developments of the person, this search for identity we are talking about.

BURRIS: It's a big question.

MEDINA: Do you want me to make it smaller?

BURRIS: No, no, I'll deal with it. [*audience laughter*]

MEDINA: Would you like to review the expectations, Darren?

BURRIS: No, I'll rise to the expectations.

MEDINA: Don't worry if you make a mistake. [*audience laughter*]

BURRIS: I think, well, I guess it's part of my job to make math wonderful. To make it compelling and interesting even to the most resistant. I don't want to leave aside the fact that this content matters, for what it can mean in terms of some future job, or some future thing. But for it actually to be interesting, whether it be patterns or things exponentially growing, whatever it is, there are ways to make it seem curious, to get questions to come. Like, Why is it that way?

So I don't want to leave out the content. I think it's compelling. But I also think that with the new standards there is a push toward thinking that math also has all of these other habits around it, like perseverance. Actually, though, part of being a great mathematician is persevering. So when you have a problem, you try one thing, then you might try another, and you might try another, and so on, with the content on one side. That's something that I would want all my students to leave my classroom with, right? This ability to just persevere. Another one is to see structure. One of the great things in math is that you begin to see things differently, begin to see patterns, begin to put things together that you wouldn't normally put together, that you might not normally do. I'd want to bequeath that to them, that when they look at the world, that whether it's numbers are not, they're beginning to look at it carefully, to think about it. One of the goals, actually, is to construct arguments and have valid reasoning.

So whatever the content is in my math class, I want my students to be standing tall, constructing arguments, justifying their claims, constructing them in such a way that, wherever they are, they're confident, able students. Whether they're in math class or they've decided not to do anything with math and they're in law school, that's something I think a math class can get—

HOLTZ: Excuse me, Darren, is that going to help my kids' standardized test scores?

BURRIS: I did mention the content part at the beginning; I do get to that, too.

HOLTZ: Well, how do you test for this stuff? And I'm only semi-joking here. How do you test for the fact that kids are becoming more effective thinkers, that they can put an argument together? Like in geometry, right? Boom, boom, boom.

BURRIS: Well, I guess I would ask, Do we have to assess that?

HOLTZ: All other legislators out there are saying, If you're teaching it in the classroom, it better be something that you can test for, because your salary is gonna depend on it, too, if your kids do poorly. And I'm not joking on that one, right?

BURRIS: No, and I think that's one of the things we're talking about today. The topic of this, our discussion, is about where we want the future of U.S. education to go, and what it means for identity. I think that right now, when a teacher walks into a room, and they're thinking about themselves and the course and these kids as, do they know whatever's going to be covered on the April exam? That for me is still an important part of what education does, giving kids knowledge, or creating experiences where they gain knowledge. But because over the last 15 years that's become the sole focus, I would hope that in the next 15 we realize that a kid doesn't persevere and finish their college degree because they learned X and they got this score, but rather because they learned something about themselves and learned how to deal with failure, they learned how to organize themselves, manage their time. They want to believe in themselves. Those, all of those things, make for an effective education system. So I wouldn't disagree with you.

MEDINA: Which is interesting, because at the end of the day even we educators within us have this craving for education. I heard you say something like: "a very high-risk business." But we want to also be accountable to ourselves and to our kids, so therefore we want also to measure it.

If we actually want to communicate to our kids that they're making a mistake, we have to show them that they made it. And we are in between these worlds, in which ultimately we want these kids to flourish and become something we cannot yet imagine them to be. Yet, at the same time, we wonder, How are we getting there? To what extent are we...

When you two think about what your classroom looks like, how you treat your students—how does that reflect to the culture of your faculty? As you were saying, I want to be a model of a learner, no? What we are asking the students to do in the classroom and in the hallways—do we have different expectations for the adults there?

BURRIS: I would say that early on I thought that I knew I had sufficient knowledge skills, even to do the job well. And that it was my job to... get the students to get on board with my plan for them. But as you know, when we started three or four years ago, working together as schools in Boston, well, when you start teaching you realize that you're not sufficient yourself. If you're really trying to do right by the students you have each year, I think that you begin to model the kind of learning that you want in your kids. You know that where you are now is not where you need to be, that you will need help, you will need people observing you, you'll need people looking at your lessons, you need people helping you all along the way. That's one of the reasons why my little school down the street came to your building, and I started working with your math teachers. I watched their classrooms, they watched mine; we started thinking together, because I wasn't sufficient myself. I had to learn about what I was doing. I think a culture of learning like that, if it's happening among the staff, is much different when you get to the kids because you start to see them as learners, you're all learners. It sounds a little *Kumbaya*-ish, but it is pretty wonderful. I mean—

HOLTZ: *Kumbaya* is a great song.

BURRIS: Yeah. [*audience laughter*]

MEDINA: Final question. Fr. Holtz, if adults basically allow me this space to grow and to, in a sense, make decisions, to be free, and in being free decide a structure that allows me to risk, to make mistakes, to be corrected—is that enough, or do I need to belong somewhere? Ultimately, do I really need a group of people around me, do I need to belong to somebody, in order to find this identity that I'm talking about?

HOLTZ: Well, the kids apparently think so, because the gang movement in Newark—we're in the Bloods neighborhood, frankly. But one of the things that can get you thrown out of St. Benedict is membership in a gang. Because we only have one gang at St. Benedict's, and that's us. That's our gang, you can't belong to somebody else. That's what it's all about. We need to belong. Kids will go out and commit murder so they can belong to a gang. That's what we're built for, right? Even God, God is family. God is love; three Persons interacting, interrelating. It's part of our nature. So to build an environment in which the kids are competing against each other, and don't care about one another, that's not teaching them how to be a human being, it seems to me. Can I interject something? In our physics lab, Father Mark put up this sign: "If you can measure it, it's not that important."

BURRIS: What was the question? [*audience laughter*]

MEDINA: How important it is to belong somewhere. Successful schools these days, like your schools, tend to have a very strong identity as a school. In other words, if I were to walk around Newark, I know that I would recognize your kids. If I work in a collegiate neighborhood, if I'm in Dorchester neighborhood, I know how to distinguish the collegiate from the Cristo Rey, from the Berke kids. There is a very strong sense of identity that comes out of the fact of belonging to a place, but nevertheless there is the desire to be free.

BURRIS: I would say we have a lot less of that. We're not there yet with kids feeling like they totally belong to a place. I think some do. And I think we've done right by a collection of them. I would say that the parents and families, though, are there for the same reasons. We have a very strong college prep mission that we're going to prepare every single student for college. I think all of the kids do believe that. But I also think that we're trying to figure out if we are supposed to be all things for all those kids. Some of those kids come from very strong families, very tight-knit communities, and they're actually coming to us just for a safe place to learn. I think that, without a doubt, the kids who are most successful there are the ones that feel belonging there, that find strength there; they don't find limits, but they find strength. They find that wherever they're gonna go next, it's better for them to have been there.

I think we're still trying to figure things out. We know that we can't be everything and all things to them, and that we shouldn't be, but how do we strike that balance? How do we meet each kid's needs? How do we be what we should be for that individual kid? It's something we're still trying to work out.

MEDINA: Final question to you, too, Fr. Holtz, and this is for you to answer briefly, even though it's unfair of me to ask it that way. Another way of asking you the question of what is the heart of the schools where you work is to ask whether it can be replicated. So what is the piece that I would need to grab from what you have, in order to have what you have?

HOLTZ: What a great question!

MEDINA: I know! I prepared! [*audience laughter*]

HOLTZ: Wow. Let me email you an answer in about two days. Isn't it great, everybody's holding their breath. We don't have a program that you can, like, you can buy the St. Benedict's program, but all those different elements, people can pick, and you can have kids run your school, but it'll take some time to do that. So there are different elements, but I suppose one of the real big ones, for me, anyway, is "Whatever hurts my brother hurts me."

To get the kids to believe that, we hook them together on the Appalachian Trail. The first day they walk in, they belong to what we call the color group. My group is purple, and there are seven of us. And one's a black guy—well, a couple of black kids; a Hispanic kid; and the funky white boys, we call 'em. [*audience laughter*] Kid from Mongolia. Whatever hurts my brother hurts me, and whatever hurts me hurts my brother. Whatever helps my brother helps me. Hmmm.

If you can get them to believe that, then they're gonna be good fathers, who aren't going to walk out on their spouses and children. They're gonna be good citizens. Who knows what else they can be?

BURRIS: I think it's hard for structures. I mean, even though structures seem the easiest thing to transition, like...I'm thinking about bringing back this idea of having 7th through 12 grade advisories, maybe, pulling that structure from your context, and seeing what it would be like in my school. But I think for us it's more about the disposition of continuous improvement. It's very easy to go in every day and to try to not be better the next day. I think the school will change in ten years, it will be different. Five years ago it was a very different place.

So the only thing that I would say I would want someone to take off the shelf, if they were going to replicate the school, is to say, How are you always going to insure that you are not settled, that you haven't settled for "good enough"? And I think one way that we do that is to have a flat structure, where any changes in the school are led from teachers, or led from the rank and file, from teachers, and so there's committees for teacher retention, there are committees for college readiness, there are committees on race and diversity, so that when the school decides to take a new direction, it's not anybody else but the teachers making that decision. It's a continuous improvement, and its improvement based on we've owned, that this is where we wanna go. That's what you should take.

MEDINA: Thank you very much, the two of you. Two very particular schools. One is run by teachers, and the other one is run by students. Not everything is as pretty as described, but what is very true of both of them is that they're two schools where the communities are very much eager to help people learn, and not to protect them. Eager to be open, and to allow the kids to explore, to make mistakes, to get up and stand, to keep moving. Adults who actually believe that the only difference between us and the kids is that we are more mature because we've learned more, therefore, we've grown more.

Thank you very much, Father Holtz and Darren. If you want an out before you applaud, Father Holtz brought a couple of books, one that he wrote and one that describes what the urban school culture is in his school. I talked him into selling them, not giving them away for free, because these schools don't run themselves.

You can actually buy them in the back from Human Adventure Books. I'll have him sign it, or you can talk to him. Thank you very much. Thank you.

SPENCER
WATERS

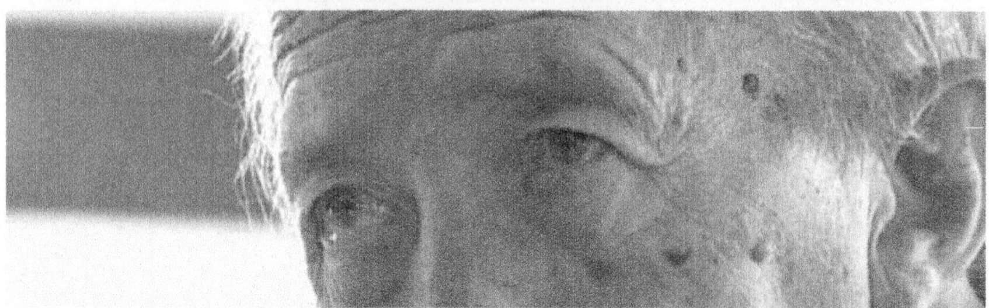

WATERS
SPENCER
SHANKMAN
WATERS

"May You Never Be Content" – Msgr. Luigi Giussani's Legacy

Eyewitness accounts of Fr. Giussani's life, commemorating the 10th anniversary of his death by ***Elizabeth Peralta****, student at Saint Francis College,* ***Kim Shankman****, Dean of Benedictine College,* ***Archibald Spencer****, Professor of Theology, Northwest Baptist Theological Seminary, Canada, and* ***John Waters****, journalist*

Introduction

"Christ, this is the name that indicates and defines a reality I have encountered in my life. I have encountered: I heard of it when I was a child, as a boy, and so on. It is possible to grow up knowing the word "Christ" well, but for many people He is not encountered. He is not really experienced as being present. In my case, Christ "bumped into" my life, my life "bumped into" Christ, precisely, so that I should learn to understand that He is the central point of everything, of the whole of my life.
Christ is the life of my life.

In Him is summed up all that I would desire, all that I look for, all that I sacrifice, all that develops in me out of love for the people with whom He put me, that is, out of love for you. As Moeller said in a sentence I have quoted many times, "I think I could no longer live if I no longer heard Him speak". Perhaps is one of the sentences I've remembered most in my life."

Luigi Giussani, 1997

Sunday, January 18, 2015

❖ ❖ ❖ ❖ ❖

JOHN WATERS: Good morning. My name is John Waters, I'm from Ireland. It's a great joy to be here today to mark and celebrate the 10th anniversary of Fr. Giussani's death. We start this morning with a short video, only six minutes, and then we'll continue our discussion.

[Video Presentation]

WATERS: "May you never be content, may you never be tranquil." It sounds like an Irish curse. [*audience laughter*] But I hope that after an hour's time we'll have convinced each other that actually it's the direct opposite. We have three speakers here today. On my left is Elizabeth Peralta; on my right is Kimberly Shankman; then Archie Spencer on my extreme right. No significance intended. Each will speak for 15 minutes. And then we will wrap up.

Remembering Giussani in this, the 10th anniversary of that year, and being in New York, it's also impossible not to remember Lorenzo Albacete, whom I first met in Rimini in 2006. And what an extraordinary witness he was to the charism of Giussani, in his personality, and in his humor and vivacity. I had lunch with him: and when you go to Rimini for the first time, one of the things you encounter is that nobody wants to have lunch with you. Lorenzo had lunch with me, for which I'm eternally grateful to him. But there are memories of him everywhere in New York. I was struck. I was about to read these biographies, and was reminded of an incident the last time I was here. Lorenzo was introducing a panel like this, and when he got to this point, he realized that he didn't have the biographies in front of him.

So then he, resourceful as ever, said, "Well, of course, it will be an insult to these speakers if I was to introduce them." [*audience laughter*]

And then, almost immediately, somebody sprang from the midst of the crowd with a sheet of paper, and left it in front of Albacete. And he looked at it ruefully, and said, "And now they are going to be insulted." [*audience laughter*]

So I propose to insult each of these speakers in turn, and they will speak for 15 minutes and then we'll continue.

Our first speaker is Archie Spencer, Associate Professor in the John H. Pickford Chair in Theology at Northwest Baptist Seminary in Canada. Dr. Spencer's education includes degrees from Regent College, and University of Toronto School of Theology. At Associated Canada Theological schools, Dr. Spencer is actively engaged in teaching, presentations, and thesis supervision in the fields of Systematic, Philosophical, Historical, and Ecumenical Theology.

He also teaches in the undergraduate Department of Religious Studies at Trinity Western University, where he is Associate Professor of Theology. His research interests include Contemporary Theology in the Western Tradition, the Theology of Karl Barth, Eberhard Jüngel, Reformation and Evangelical Theology, and Alexandrian Theology of the first three centuries.

He has published a major work on the theology of Karl Barth, and has written numerous academic articles, reviews, chapters, and popular articles, some of which have been translated into other languages. His most recent publication, *Analogy of Faith: The Christological Content of Theology*, is forthcoming from Intervarsity Press, later this year, I think. Archie Spencer.

ARCHIE SPENCER: Thank you very much, John, and thank you all for being here today and sharing with us in this wonderful opportunity to remember and celebrate the legacy of Don Giussani, as the 10th anniversary of his going home to be with his Lord approaches. It is for me an absolute honor to be invited to speak at such a moment. Giussani's impact on my life has, well, yet to be finally estimated. It won't be estimated until my life is over; it is an ongoing impact.

Let me just give you a sense of why Giussani was so important for me, by giving you a bit of background in the context of my life. I was born on a smallish rock in the middle of the North Atlantic that was covered with snow and ice for eight months of the year. Looking down at the right time, you would assume that I was born on an iceberg with swinging doors. But, the narrow confines of my home were only partially matched by the absolutely narrow confines of the political, social, and religious upbringing that was mine. When we met Catholics in the street, and they were rare, by the way—a species from another planet—we were reminded that these were the deepest, most dyed-in-the-wool sinners that existed on the face of the earth; candidates for conversion, which we should immediately set about doing. And if they refused to do it within half an hour, then find the nearest boat to ship them off the island. The attitudes were that narrow. So of course for me it was with that kind of education that I proceeded to go and do theological studies. Slowly but surely I had my mind opened to other possibilities, until towards the end of my doctoral studies—and here I'm beginning to answer the first of the questions: How did I come to encounter Giussani?

In 1998, just towards the end of my doctorate examination period, I was an adjunct at a given college in upper Canada, McMaster Divinity College. The editor of our journal threw a book on my desk and said, "Here, review this for the next edition of the journal." I said, "I don't have time," and he said, "You don't have a choice." So I immediately set about reading *The Religious Sense*, only to discover to my absolute amazement that it was a treatment of religion on the order of Immanuel Kant, Schleiermacher, Hegel, and all of the greats that had written major treatises on religion. The impression was immediately deep. The review caught the attention of the original editor and translator of that book, John Zucchi, and John invited me to come to Montreal in 2002, and then subsequently in 2003 after doing a presentation on *Why the Church?*

I was invited to Italy for the first time to speak at Rimini, and let me tell you, that moment remains an indelible moment in my life. Not just because of the friends that I met there, the opportunity I had to engage people in significant ways, but because also, in the graciousness of his heart—given the illnesses he was struggling with at the time—Don Giussani, Fr. Giussani, Msgr. Giussani, invited me to his home for lunch. The meeting was, to say the least, absolutely astounding to me. I did not know at first how to present myself to him, so I decided humility was absolutely the order of the day. To put aside the narrow confines of my upbringing and admit that I, too, was a sinner. So my introduction to him was, "Fr. Giussani, I hope you will receive me; I'm just a poor Protestant sinner." And he said to me, "Only if you will receive me, a poor Catholic priest who is an even bigger sinner." Thus confirming my education up to that point. [*audience laughter*]

But the interesting thing about that was, he and I found ourselves in the same condition before God. And this was the Giussani I met. The man whose expansive mind and heart and spirit were able to enfold me and include me in his love in an instant. And before I left the table, which was some two, three hours, I can't remember—he knew my whole life. He had penetrated through to the core of my being. He had made me laugh, made me cry, made me sigh, made me long for God. And that, my friends, was probably the most significant moment in my movement from the narrow confines of my home and upbringing to an openness and an expansiveness in respect to the grace of God.

So, now to the second question: What influence has this had on my life today? Every encounter we have with individuals, as with the encounter with Christ, is never exhausted in the moment of the encounter, but rather is a constant encounter for the rest of your life, even when you're absent from them; because to know and to be known is a lifetime endeavor based on the fullness of being that's presented to you within every encounter. And so here are the areas that have changed my life most significantly. Friendship. Not only do I have more friends, through my connections with CL, but I have a greater degree and capacity for friendship because of my encounter and reading of Giussani.

An expanded vision of grace. Understanding now that the narrow confines of my upbringing and my religious views need the wideness and openness of God's grace. Giussani came at the end of my doctoral studies as a final confirmation that the Church was bigger than my upbringing.

A humanum that surpasses all humanity; a fullness of being and identity in myself and in Christ that is included in the fullness of the way in which God deals with us. This came through in Giussani's anthropology on a regular basis. And then an anticipation of greater encounter. I don't think Giussani's charism is spent. I think that it will continue for a very, very long time. So the fullness of the legacy of Giussani can only be measured by looking around you at the moment, and will be so much more meaningful 20 years, 30 years, 50 years from now, should the Lord tarry. Thank you very much. [*audience applause*]

WATERS: Thank you very much, Archie. Our next speaker is Kimberly Shankman, who is the dean of Benedictine College in Atchison, Kansas. She received her PhD in Political Science from Northern Illinois University. Subsequently she taught in the Politics and Government Department at Ripon College from 1985-2001, when she left to take her current position at Benedictine College.

Her research interests are American political thought and constitutional law. She is the author of *Compromise and the Constitution: The Political Thought of Henry Clay*. Additionally, she has published articles relating to the privileges or immunities clause of the 14th amendment, and other aspects of constitutional law. Her recent scholarship focuses on the relationship between reason and public life, including the papers *Truth and Democracy*, presented at the University of the Sacred Heart in Milan, Italy; *Human Capital in* Caritas in Veritate, at Columbia University in New York; *What the Catholic Church Demands of Those in Power*, for the Crossroads Cultural Center in New York; and *Reason, Truth, and Democracy: Pope Benedict on Public Life*, at the University of St. Thomas in Houston. Kimberly Shankman. [*audience applause*]

KIM SHANKMAN: I'm going to start my presentation by frankly admitting in the first place that I never met Fr. Giussani, and in the second place that I don't understand Fr. Giussani. As a matter of fact, what springs to my mind is this: when I was in graduate school, I spent a semester in England, and one day shortly after I got there, there was a cricket match on TV. I love baseball, so I thought, Oh, I'll watch this, and I'll figure it out. And so I watched the cricket match. At first it was kind of chaotic, yet I saw a pattern emerging. But then they'd do something completely unexpected. They'd start running the other way, or everyone would sit down, or something like that. So for me, to read Fr. Giussani's works is like watching cricket. [*audience laughter*] Every time I think I know where he's going, something completely unexpected happens.

But I'm very grateful because I was actually introduced to the Movement through the people of the Movement. One of the monks at our abbey, St. Benedict's Abbey in Atchison, Kansas, invited Msgr. Albacete to Atchison, so he was my first introduction to the Movement. Then some other members came and started a *Memores Domini* house in Kansas. I used to say to myself, I don't understand a word this man says, but every single person I've met who is involved with this Movement is, I would say, incredibly nice. But, you know, I know a lot of nice people. All through my life people have been nice to me whatever happened, so it was more than that they were just nice. It was interesting, but it also provoked me. We started a School of Community in Atchison, and I would go and try to understand what I was—it would provoke me to ask the question: What am I looking for? What am I trying to find? Sometimes the provocation really bothered me a lot. I remember a couple of years ago—the year that we were basically concentrating on the concept of the positivity of reality. There was a letter to Fr. Carrón published in *Traces* from a social worker in a hospital who had interacted with a woman who'd tried for years and years to get pregnant; and then shortly after she got pregnant she was diagnosed with cancer. So she was very depressed, and upset, and suffering; and the social worker wrote to Fr. Carrón: "Because of Don Giussani's understanding of the positivity of reality, I am able to interact with this woman in a way that I can see the positivity of it." And I left that school of community, and I just wrestled in my mind. I said, "This is horrible, to think that God would make this poor woman suffer like this, essentially as a job training exercise." It just seemed horrible to me to think of that. And I wrestled with it in my mind for months.

But usually the provocation was more along the lines of something I saw in people and knew was more than I had in my life. I remember at an Advent retreat we had on our campus one of our students, whose sister, a former student of ours, was engaged in a particularly courageous battle with cancer. He got up and sort of gave a little testimony and was talking about how he had come to accept and support this, and what he said was—what struck me about what he said was, "I know she doesn't belong to me. She belongs to another who loves her more than I do."

And I thought, I could never, ever, be like that. I could never be that open, I could never be that accepting, I could never be that strong. So I was just in awe and thought, Maybe I'm not good enough to be part of this group. I still wanted to be there, though, because there were people like that there.

And then, just a few weeks after that, my son, my 17-year-old son—it was the day after Pope Francis was elected. It was a beautiful spring day, so my son and his friends thought the right thing to do was to get in the back of a pickup truck and go joyriding in the park. Their friend was not a very experienced driver, and so the truck hit a mud patch; it flipped. Most of the boys, thankfully—actually all the boys except for John, my son—were only slightly injured: cuts and bruises. But John suffered an extremely serious, traumatic brain injury, along with many additional injuries. That event changed my life in an incredibly dramatic way. There were three moments related to that event that, in my engagement with the Movement, really meant a lot to me in the immediate aftermath.

The first was, by the time we got to the scene of the accident, the police called, I was at work, I had to go get my husband, we got to the scene of the accident, and the helicopter had already left. He was being life-flighted to the regional medical center, University of Kansas Hospital, so we had to drive down there. The emergency responders didn't know if he was still alive. We didn't know if he was going to be alive when we got down there; we didn't know what to expect. And so of course we were afraid, we were worried, we were just frantic. And those words that that student had said came back to us. I said to Don, my husband, "He doesn't belong to us. He belongs to another who loves him more than we can." And, when I could say that, when we could say that, it changed everything. Of course, we were still worried, we were still unsure, we were still frantic in a certain way, but there was a peace, a strength there that made the whole experience different. It changed everything.

I'm going to tell you another moment. They told us that if he made it through the first 48 hours, he had a good chance of surviving. So, we're counting down the clock, and he gets to 48 hours, and whew, yeah, he made it. But then, six days later, six days after the accident—his accident was on a Thursday, this was a Wednesday morning—we were staying at a hotel across the street from the hospital so we could come in early in the morning, check on him, go have breakfast, then come back and spend the day with him. Well, when we came in that morning, he was lethargic. It turned out that the pressure was building again in his brain. And this was the first time his neurosurgeon, who is a wonderful man, told us that he was not sure that John would survive the day. He said there's one more thing I can try, and we said yes, go for it! Three times they told us there was nothing more they could do, four times Dr. Camarata came up with something out of his bag of tricks. So he took him down for this emergency surgery, and as he left, we watched John being wheeled away. This was a Wednesday morning. During those first 48 hours we'd had people with us all the time. We thought, this is going to be really different this time because we're here alone. It's Wednesday morning, everyone's at work, we're just here. We walked out into the waiting room, and all of a sudden, the Abbott from our monastery walked in, and I said, "Barnabas, what are you doing here?"

"Well, you know, Dr. Camarata had done surgery on my spine last summer, and I was supposed to have a checkup today, but I got to his office and they told me he was in emergency brain surgery." That's us! And so he was there. And then Salvatore and Daniel, *Memores Domini*, walked in; other friends from our School of Community came in; it was the Wednesday miracle. And why I say this was a miracle is because we didn't even know that we needed this companionship. We didn't know what to pray for. We were praying for Johnny, but God knew what we needed at that time were companions. And that changed everything.

And then the final thing, the final moment where the meeting had this impact on my life, was: after the surgery, they had him in an induced coma, and so we went home. We came back a few days later when it was time to wake him up. It was time to move from this kind of real emergency to a more long-term program of care, so they had to insert a feeding tube, a tracheostomy, and so forth. We had this care meeting first. He had actually not awakened from the coma since the accident, so the palliative care doctor said to us, "You need to think about whether he would want to live this way. We don't have to do these things, we don't have to go forward. We don't have to take these measures. Think about whether he would want to live this way."

I was so grateful because I realized in that moment that I didn't have to give a logical argument based on the teachings of the Church and so forth, about what needed to happen. I could say what I said, which was, "We love our son laying in that bed, right now, and if the rest of his life is to lay in that bed, we will love him for the rest of his life. Of course he wouldn't want to live this way. No sane person would want to live this way. But his choice is not between living that way and living the way he used to live. This is the life that God has now given him, and this life is not ours to give or take away. This life is a gift, and it is his. And so we are going forward."

I just felt so grateful that I was able to have that kind of clarity and make that kind of statement.

I now see how, yes, my son's suffering is real, he still can't walk, he can't talk, he can't turn himself over in bed, he's totally dependent for his care; but his suffering is not my problem. His suffering belongs to Christ. He has some mysterious relationship with Christ now that is not mine to figure out. But the positive things—he's taught me what real poverty means. It's the fact that if I had all the money in the world I couldn't buy what I want the most, which is his return to health. But what I can do is what's in front of me: love him every day. These good things have made a beggar out of me. Everyone I meet I tell, "Please pray for my son." He's made me understand what it means to receive charity. Our neighbors came together. The contractors in town donated their labor so that we could build an addition to our house so we could bring him home. All of those things are good. He turns people into the hands and feet of Christ, people who come to visit him, people who come to watch the Packers game with him, the CLU at Benedictine College who come and sing with him every couple of weeks. His friends, who are just teenage boys, you know? Teenage boys, they'll come and spend a couple hours with him, just to be with him. The hands and feet of Christ: people have the chance to do that.

I have to say, though, I still can't understand Fr. Giussani. I can't define for you what experience means, what judgment means. I'm not even sure I can tell you what "I" means [*audience laughter*]. But I do know that my son is a witness to the positivity of reality. His suffering and what has happened to him, it's not a good thing in itself, but it has brought so much good and it has helped me so much. I don't know, I don't think I would have been able to understand this if I hadn't met the Movement, if I hadn't had this education that brought me to the point where I could understand this. I'm very grateful for the charism that Fr. Giussani passed on to those who carry it with them and bring it to the world. Thank you. [*audience applause*]

WATERS: Thank you, Kimberly. Our final speaker is Elizabeth Peralta, who is a graduate from Port Chester Senior High School in Westchester, New York. She is currently in her last year studying History and English at St. Francis College in Brooklyn Heights. Elizabeth Peralta.

ELIZABETH PERALTA: Hello, everybody. I didn't meet Giussani, either, just to clarify, but a couple months ago I found myself in a hospital room sitting next to Albacete. To be honest, afterwards I was really scared, because it reminded me of my mother. But afterwards I realized that Albacete gave me the memory again of why Christ is literally the most beautiful thing to have ever happened to me. Out of the many jokes that Albacete made, because I'm sure you all know him, he said three things that I'll never forget.

The first thing he said was—because I tried to promise him that I would come back to see him that weekend, and he assured me that I wouldn't be able to because he was going to sneak on a plane to Puerto Rico and go back—"Don't worry, because even if I'm not here next to you, I'm always with you. I'm suffering with you, we're suffering together."

It's true, because in high school, right before I met the Movement, I remember just being really sad and desperate. Especially because I had a really big fight with my friend, and this was the friend that I turned to for everything. After that, I started partying and drinking alcohol, and doing a lot of other things. But nothing was enough anymore. I felt really numb, and yet my friend, with whom I'd had the fight—even though I was considered "cool" and she was considered a "loser"—I asked her one day, "Why are you so happy? Like, what drugs are you taking, 'cause I want them." And she was like, "I'm not taking any drugs. I'm going to School of Community." My last experience of School of Community had been some kind of thing where you talk about Jesus, and I was like, I really don't want to talk about Jesus, but I'll go, because my goal was to regain her friendship.

I ended up going, but the whole School of Community I was on my phone, texting. Every time I heard "Jesus" I'm pretty sure I rolled my eyes. But then something struck me because somebody was there and it was a boy. He was talking about the pain he felt because his father had to go back to Colombia. I remember dropping my phone and kicking it across the room, saying, "If God exists, then why did my father leave?"—because this has always been a really big pain for me. My father left when I was six, and I guess I had always blamed myself for that.

Then this woman I didn't even know, she looked at me and said something I'll never forget. She said, "I can't give you an answer, but I can promise to suffer with you." In high school I found so many things that made me feel good, but they never lasted. I had many friends, but they were the "go out and party, get drunk" kind of friends. Not one had said they would suffer with me.

The second thing that Albacete told me was to remember that there is no happiness, sadness, or any emotion without the Church, because it is here where the Father is found. After that moment at School of Community, I continued to follow the Movement. So much so that I went on a vacation and found myself in front of a room full of people I didn't even know, asking, "I'm here to know what it means to love and to be loved." After that I became a member of the CLU, which is the CL university students, and I followed that way. My questions remained about my father. It was weird, because he even got in contact with me. But every time we'd arrange to meet, I ended up sitting at a restaurant alone, waiting, and he never showed; he always had an excuse. Every time I was in this sadness, this woman that I didn't even know—I later found out that her name was Camil, she was in *Memores Domini*—she was keeping her promise from the first time. She promised that she would suffer with me, and she did. One time she said, "Liz, I don't want to repeat this, but I think it's important that you do your sacraments, because it's the ultimate dialog with Christ."

And of course I didn't really listen, because I never listen the first time. My dad contacted me again, but he didn't show, and this time it really hurt. This time I found myself in front of the cross in a room, begging and saying, "Christ, if you exist then why do I feel so alone?" I can't really explain it, but I just felt this really huge embrace. I picked up the phone and called Fr. Rich and began traveling from the Upper East Side to Staten Island every Saturday at 8:00 a.m. to do CCD. Why? It was because I wanted to find the father. Because I began to realize that I needed more than ideas about my father to be happy. And also because through that embrace, which I can't really explain, I realized that my father had always been with me. He was just waiting for my yes.

The third thing was that Albacete asked me where I was from, and of course I said, "Well, my mom is Dominican, but I'm from New York." And he looked at me, and he yelled at me and said, "But? Why are you saying but?" And I was like, "What do you mean?" And he's like, "Don't ever be ashamed of where you are from. Say: My mom is Dominican, and I am from New York." Then he ended by saying, "Embrace everything!"

It's weird to think of that last sentence, "Embrace everything," because for a long time I felt like I was part of the Movement, yet felt as if [the order of my life's priority's] was my life in the Movement, then school, then friends. I remember the Way of the Cross, walking across the Brooklyn Bridge, realizing that, if the love that is here in the Movement is true, then it has to be true with even my mother with whom I'd always had a very difficult time; because if you know Hispanic women, it's really hard to get along with them. After a certain amount of time it's like, okay, if this is true, I have to bring it to my mother, and I did. I began sharing Christ and the Movement with her. One night she looked at me with tears in her eyes and said, "That gaze that you talk about, the love that you talk about, that's what I've wanted my whole life." Embracing the Movement means embracing Christ. Through Christ I learned that my heart is the same as my mother's, making the last year of her life the most beautiful one I shared with her.

To go into reality is painful, and I am suffering a lot more than I did before. It's not like, because I met the Movement, everything, like, all my problems went away. Meeting the Movement made reality so much more thick. Being a student, this meant more than just getting good grades. It meant loving my family differently. It made falling in love differently, because I was facing a reality that was not easy, not immediately beautiful. But all of this helped me to ask, What is the real beauty of life if it's not the circumstance? Even though I never met Giussani, when I went to his tomb last year, a couple of weeks after my mom passed away, I just stood in front of his tomb and my heart was so alive. I realized that this man gave me a place where I could look at my heart, where I could face the questions that everyone else always told me to ignore, and helped me to understand my belonging, not only to CL but to Christ. Thank you. [*audience applause*]

WATERS: Thank you, Elizabeth. See what happens when we talk about this man? We go immediately to the center of everything. We're not taken through all the small talk, all the details, all the peripherals—we just go right to the heart of our lives, the meaning of everything straightaway, with each other. We meet in the street and we start talking not about the weather, but about life, about reality. This is the first of these gifts to us. And Archie talked about the expanse of the heart and mind and spirit of Giussani. Which is of course, a great, great human quality. But the thing about Giussani that strikes me so often is that, what other figure—can you imagine another figure who could inspire us to sit in rooms, talking at such depth about life, being moved, laughing, with such an intensity, with such friendliness, with such openness, 10 years after his death? And it grows, it grows, it grows. What politician, what writer, what artist, anybody, in all of these areas of life, in every area of life? We talk about this man because it seems to me his humanity was great; but more, he's like a booster unit or something for our feeble stabs, our uncertainties in trying to find something: he picks up our signal and he boosts it to somewhere else. He connects us to somewhere else. Through his personality and his work and his humanity we are connected to the infinite, learning how to grow again into the fullness of the humanity that was given us in the first bit, but which for all kinds of reasons has become subdued and suppressed.

I was walking back to the hotel last night with Rose, my hostess, and I was just looking around at Manhattan, reflecting on my own feelings of being here. Because being here in New York should be for me an experience that overcomes me in every instance. I should be overwhelmed. I was overwhelmed the first time. In a month's time, I will go back and think, I was in New York. What happened? I didn't really do it justice. It reminds me of walking along and—a friend of mine has an expression: I didn't know whether—looking at New York—I didn't know whether to eat it, drink it, or sleep with it. [*audience laughter*] That's the sanitized version. [*audience laughter*]

There's something in me that's expecting something that isn't quite there, and this is the story of my life. I thought it was just a random circumstance until I started to read Giussani and saw that it was the way he connected it into everything. He connected back to the days when I was a child, first, an altar boy kneeling before the altar, looking, hearing these stories. Everything became connected to this desire. So it wasn't an accident. Nothing was an accident. It was all here [*puts hand on heart*]. There's a story in the world that I belong to, that is me. Giussani explains it, and he explains everything that ever happened to me, every feeling I ever had, every thought I ever couldn't work out, every contradiction in me. He seemed to be there, watching me. This is an amazing, amazing thing.

I didn't meet Giussani, I only heard of him. I heard of him on the—this morning, actually, in my hotel room, I told a story of how I first encountered somebody from Communion and Liberation in the airport of Dublin on my way to Rome in 2005. It was to mark my 50th birthday. It was actually a few days after my birthday, the third of June, 2005. It was a Friday. And the third of June—I never made the connection before this morning—the third of June is a very meaningful day in my life: it's the date my father died in 1989. I never really connected that the day I first heard of Giussani was the same day, the same date that my father died. And that to me has a huge resonance, a sign for me of something great.

When you go into this story, into this experience, you find these little things all the time. Suddenly your life has stopped being random and chaotic, and becomes an ordered something. A convergence, a path converging in front of you. The role that I was speaking of yesterday, that seems to be such a theme of this year's conference—we are all poor wayfaring strangers walking along that road, heading towards the horizon, heading towards some destination that we can only vaguely intuit. We use all of these common experiences and memories and witnesses and stories to keep us going along that path.

The paradox of that journey is captured in that phrase, "May you never be content." Don't expect to be content. If you're not content, you're okay. It's not wrong. There is nothing wrong with you. You're supposed to be sad. Why wouldn't you be sad, when you're missing something so great? How will you not be sad? This is really the story of the strange paradox of life: we move through it but don't belong to it. We're going through somewhere which is, in a certain sense, alien to us; this existence, moving through it. A journey heading towards the horizon, looking for that bridge—again, another symbol of New York Encounter. The bridge that will take us over that river, over to the infinite, the world beyond.

Giussani makes all of this commonsensical. He makes it like something you would read in a different kind of newspaper than the one we would read. If we had newspapers that talked about reality as it actually is, really, then this is the stuff that would be in it. It would be newspapers talking about our desire, our hope, and our expectations; our nature, our structure, all of this. Giussani gives us this kind of guide to the everyday. It's not a separate reality, it's the real reality.

Pope Benedict XVI, whom we all loved, and love, who is five years younger than Giussani—nobody really talked about this when he was Pope, but I think Benedict was a great follower of Giussani. He was also a follower and was guided, like so many of us, by this charism. You can read it right through all of his writings. But in 2011 he gave us a really graphic image, the bunker: the bunker that man has built for himself to live in, in which he has closed out the Mystery. This is really a Giussanian concept. It's almost a concept that you add on to Giussani, it's the point that Giussani was really trying to describe in our culture, which causes us to lose sight of ourselves. Because we build a safe place, and we inhabit this and it's warm and it's safe and it's secure and it's understandable, it's comprehensible to us. We understand everything about it, we know what the temperature is, and all the things that will happen, and we can predict things. So we're not afraid anymore in this bunker, or at least we're relatively less afraid. But it shuts out the Mystery, and because it shuts out the Mystery it shuts out us. So when you read more and more into this bunker culture, you try to get to the bottom of things, about why we are as we are, why I am as I am. The only explanation is that there is something wrong with me, there's something deficient about me. I haven't understood something about the way the world works. There is a wonderful exhibition upstairs, "The Millennium Generation", which really addresses this question through the eyes of my daughter's generation, those kids born in the vicinity of the millennium. Who seem to have rumbled this whole thing. They are beginning to understand that they've been sold a pop, that they've been misled. They're being promised that everything is obvious, that everything is clear, that everything will be explained, everything will be satisfied. And yet, they can find none of this satisfaction. None of these explanations are satisfactory. Giussani told us all this and he described it. I understand Kimberly's point about—I've gotten this response many times: I'd give people Giussani's books, and they'd say, "Well, we didn't get very far." And I'd say, Well, you know, it's all right. You don't have to read it all in the one day. You can read it a paragraph at a time. You can read it a hundred times and maybe on the 99th time, that's the time you'll understand something that you never did before, or remember something you had forgotten about yourself. That's the great beauty of Giussani's charism: that he's really telling us things we already know, that we've experienced already; he's putting them together for us, before our eyes. It's not that he's taking some alien ideology or theology or doctrine and asking us to learn it by heart. He's giving us our own experience in new words and inviting us to bring even newer words to it. He used that method. If anybody was in that situation of reading Giussani and being baffled by him, I would say, get the English edition of *The Religious Sense*, go to page 100, and read that page. There's a paragraph there that really is almost the answer to Pope Benedict's analysis of our society in the bunker. Giussani gives us the method to come out of that bunker in every moment. Imagine you're just being born. Imagine that you're coming out of your mother's womb, with all of your intelligence, your knowledge, your memories, your intuition, your emotions, everything. Look, look in front of you. Look at what you see. Look at what's in front of your eyes. What are your responses? How do you respond to this? This movement, this color, this light, this everything—who are these people? And Giussani said that astonishment, wonder—this is the only natural response you can have.

And you'll have a second thought: I didn't make this. I'm not making this. I'm not making myself. This is Giussani's great gift to us. It really is a gift beyond price. Imagine, I'm 59 years of age: I was in my mid-50s before I began to see the world that is in front of me in this way. That's an astonishing thing for me to admit.

Ten years on, usually when somebody dies, 10 years is a marker: it's the beginning of forgetting. With Giussani, we know it's the beginning of remembering, because the gift he has given us is not something sentimental, not something interesting. The gift he's given us is the understanding of ourselves, of our lives, of our world. So thank you very much for coming to this, and thanks to our speakers who have been so wonderful today.

I just want to finish today with a little remembrance of Albacete, who was somebody who followed Giussani. He explained Giussani to me that day in Rimini in such a vivid way, with stories. Really impish, funny stories, irreverent stories which really—I'd never seen anything like this man before. I remember him telling me about moralism, how Giussani said that moralism was idolatry. Which is really good news for an Irish Catholic. [*audience laughter*] The first time I came to New York Encounter, I came to an event in which he spoke, and he was actually speaking that day about this problem of moralism. Afterwards, my hostess Michelle said to me, "Why don't you come back and meet the Monsignor?" I was a little scared of him, to be honest. We had a very nice chat backstage in the old venue, and then we said we would have a coffee somewhere. He got up to go, and he got his coat and started looking around the room, and I said, "Monsignor, have you lost something?" And he said, "My hat. I can't find my hat." I said, "Hmmm, what's it like?" He said, "It's one of those furry Russian hats, very nice." Okay. I've got one—no, it's not his, I promise! And I said, "Well, it must be somewhere." I started to search. Then he called me over and said, "They're not moralists. They'd steal anything." [*audience laughter*]

Thank you very much.

NEW

FREITAS
SMITH

Searching for the Human Face Online

A conversation with ***Donna Freitas****, author and lecturer, and* ***Christian Smith****, Wm. R. Kenan Jr. Professor of Sociology, University of Notre Dame, introduced by* ***John Touhey****, on how social networks and virtual communities affect human identity*

Introduction

"Human relations, and the self-image of the human being, have been profoundly affected by the Internet and by the ease with which images of other people can be summoned to the computer screen to become the objects of emotional attention. How should we conceptualize this change, and what is its effect on the psychic condition of those most given to constructing their world of interests and relationships through the screen? Is this change as damaging as many would have us believe, undermining our capacity for real relationships and placing a mere fantasy of relatedness in their stead? Or is it relatively harmless, as unproblematic as speaking to a friend on the telephone?"

Roger Scruton, *The New Atlantis,* 2010

JOHN TOUHEY: On behalf of the New York Encounter I would like to welcome Donna Freitas and Christian Smith. Donna Freitas lectures at universities across the United States about her work with college students. Over the years she has written for national newspapers and magazines, including the *Wall Street Journal*, the *New York Times*, the *Boston Globe*, and the *Washington Post*. She received her PhD in Religion from Catholic University, and she's currently a non-resident Research Associate at the

---

Saturday, January 17, 2015

Center for Religion and Society at Notre Dame. Dr. Freitas has been a professor at Boston University in the Department of Religion, and also at Hofstra University in their Honors College. She's written children's novels for Scholastic, Harper-Collins, and FSG. In 2008, Dr. Freitas published *Sex and the Soul: Juggling Sexuality, Spirituality, Romance and Religion on America's College Campuses*, with Oxford University Press, based on her national study about how sex and faith coincide and collide in the lives of college students. Currently she is at the tail-end of collecting research for a new study about social media and how it is affecting the ways we construct identity and sense of self, how we make meaning in the world and navigate our relationships. In 2014, Dr. Freitas conducted nearly two hundred in-person interviews with college students in 13 different colleges and universities about these subjects.

Christian Smith is the William R. Kenan, Jr. Professor of Sociology and Director of the Center for the Study of Religion and Society at the University of Notre Dame. Dr. Smith's research focuses primarily on religion in modernity, adolescence, American evangelicalism, and culture.

Dr. Smith received his MA and PhD from Harvard University in 1990 and his BA from Gordon College in 1983. He was Professor of Sociology at the University of North Carolina Chapel Hill for 12 years before his move to Notre Dame. Dr. Smith's more recent work on the religious and spiritual lives of U.S. adolescents emphasizes the interplay of broad cultural influences, family socialization, and religious motivations that inform a teenager's life outcomes. Behind and contributing to the sociological emphases are the philosophical works of Charles Taylor and Alasdair MacIntyre, a critical realist philosophy of social science, and an interpretive, hermeneutical understanding of sociology. So we'd like to welcome both of our speakers today as they discuss The Search for the Human Face Online, the conversation on how social networks and virtual communities affect the human identity. Welcome again. [*audience applause*]

CHRISTIAN SMITH: Thank you very much and good afternoon to all of you. Thank you for coming out. We're honored by your interest in what we have to say, and we hope what we have to say is useful and interesting for what you're doing in your lives.

The digital revolution, the Internet, and social media, we all know, have transformed social and cultural life in the last years. A lot of things have changed. The questions we want to address here are: How might this revolution be transforming our sense of ourselves, as human beings, as human persons? How might this revolution be transforming our relationships? How might it be changing the way our young people's brains are being wired?

Some of the questions are: Are social media pernicious? Are they harmful? Is it something we should be worried about? Are social media benign? Is it really not that big of a deal? Or is the situation more ambiguous, or complicated, with a mixture of the kinds of influences going on? A deeper question, more theoretical: Is any technology only as good as its users? That is, the technology is fairly neutral, so what matters are the people who are putting the technology to use. So, how good or bad a technology is is determined essentially by its users.

Or does technology form its users? Are people formed by the technologies they use? Do technologies shape people, who they are, what they aspire to, the kind of character they have? These are underlying questions about the power of technology in human existence. As a very practical starting point, very many of us worry when we see things like the following: five people hanging out at the beach, or at a restaurant together, each one of them on an iPhone, interacting with somebody else who's not there, and all those five people are ignoring each other. That happens commonly, and it's not the end of the world, but it often troubles us. It troubles me.

Some of us are worried when we see some of the nastiness of the online discourse. Some of the comments that people leave seem to be made possible by the fact that it's very impersonal. People don't have to face each other face to face, and they can say vicious things sometimes. People like me, college professors, worry when we see students who seem literally unable to sit through one class without checking Facebook on their laptop, or checking what texts are in their iPhones. But the question is, is the digital revolution ultimately a good development? Is it something we should celebrate and be happy with that just happens to have some annoying features? Or is it somehow more ominous and destructive than that?

The 20th-century Jewish personalist philosopher, Martin Buber, said famously that all real living is meeting. All real living is meeting, that is, all authentic life is a kind of intimate encounter between an "I" and a "thou," not between an "I" and an "It." If we take Buber and say, You know, all real living is meeting, then the question becomes: Do differences in the forms—that is, the technologies of meeting, of communication—change or maybe distort or perhaps enhance human identities, human cells, human nature, human living? And if they do any of those, how do they do it, and why do they do it?

My view is that we are in the middle, probably at the early stages of this digital revolution. How it will play out, what it will mean—it's probably too early to say definitively what its effects are on us and will be on us, so I tend to be tentative with all of these things. Still, I think we all know it's important to pay attention to these matters because they're profound; to raise questions, to be aware of possible problems, to think about how, if nothing else, to use technology for human flourishing rather than the distortion of human persons in human relationships.

I go back and forth between alarmism and feeling okay. And that tells me that I think for myself. I suggest that our default position should probably be where to start, maybe not where to end up; but where to start should be to avoid both alarmism and complacency. Maybe we should be very alarmed and maybe by the time we're all a lot older we'll look back and say, Why weren't we a lot more alarmed? Why didn't we, you know, raise red flags all over the place more than we did?

But I don't know that we can say that now. Maybe things are more okay than that. But I suggest we should not begin at the extremes. I also find it helpful in my own mind to remember that, historically, most significant technological developments and innovations in modern history were met with strong initial criticisms about how harmful they would be. Things that we take for granted now or that are obsolete, whether it was the factory system, or railroads or automobiles, or subways, or radios, or televisions—when they first came out, there was all sorts of alarm about how this would disrupt human life and make things worse. Some of those criticisms were actually probably correct, and we just simply have adjusted to those harms.

But humans have also, I think, a profoundly stable nature that can adapt pretty well to environmental changes with our robust humanity intact. So you can see I'm actually of multiple minds about all this. I haven't settled in my own mind what I think about this. At the same time, however, I and many other people do have real concerns. For one thing, the larger context, the modernity, various forces and ideologies and modernity, already seriously question the very idea of a real stable, substantive human personhood.

Is there even such thing as a human person? There are lot of forces that are at work now and ideologies that call that into question. And even if these forces and ideas are false, they can be destructive when they're taken seriously. So the question we want to address here is, do social media contribute, in some sense or not, to the erosion of a thick sense of our human personhood, or of the quality of our relationships? Do social media enhance or corrode human well-being? To be clear, our goal here is not to answer all the questions, but just to raise questions to explore possible concerns, to lay out ideas of what social media may be doing to and among us, so that then we can all carry on these important reflections and conversations together. So my partner here, Donna Freitas, has been doing some fascinating social research on this very topic with college students, and I'm gonna bounce the ball over to her, and ask if she would share some of her research and her reflections and findings from that with us.

DONNA FREITAS: Well, in the vein of not answering any questions, I'm gonna present you with some data that you can chew on a little bit today. It has to do with how college students are interacting with social media. What role does it have in their lives and their self-understanding in their relationships? I want to mention briefly why I started doing this research. For the last year or so, I've been traveling around to 13 different colleges and universities in the U.S.—Catholic, Evangelical, private, secular, and public universities. Different kinds of universities all over the map. I'm sitting down and talking to college students about social media and their lives, and the reason why I decided to do this research was because of an earlier study that I did on sex and faith on college campuses. Because of that research, I spent a lot of time talking to college students all over the U.S. I visit their campuses and I usually give a lecture and I end up in conversations with them afterwards, during dinner, or just in the Q&A following my lectures. One of the things that had happened in the last couple years was I always got all kinds of interesting questions from students.

And that's how I know what they're thinking about, what's really interesting to them. Then starting probably around 2010, but in particular in 2013, I felt like everywhere I went, every student I spoke with wanted to know, What about social media? How is that affecting what people think? What do you think other college students think about social media and how we have relationships? I would get these very frenzied questions from college students, and so finally I decided, Okay, clearly the students want to know about each other, they want to know what people are thinking. That's when I did this research. It grew out of the other research.

So, given the topic of the conference, I thought I would start with just the idea of the self. One of the things I was curious about was: Where does social media—all those things you put up on Facebook and Twitter—what does it have to do with you? How is it integrated or not, into your self-understanding?

At the beginning of the interview, I ask every single student, Tell me what you think the "self" is. I just literally say, Tell me what you think the "self" is, what makes up the "self"?

And then I ask, What makes up your "self"? What makes you *you*? And this is before we get into any social media questions. I did that early on, because I wanted to know if any of the students would say in their answer, unprompted, Well, my Facebook profile is a huge part of who I am. And what was really interesting to me was that only one student, out of a 175 so far, said that. I had to push them later on and be like, Well, where does Facebook fit? Or, where do all your online profiles fit that you mentioned earlier on, when I asked you what online profiles are you committed to? That's when they would have to think about it.

So first off, college students don't seem to think about Facebook and Twitter and Instagram and Snapchat and all that stuff out there, all the time, as a fundamental part of what makes them who they are. I thought that was really interesting. There were some students, too—I asked them, "So, where do you think the 'self' is? Is it out there, in, like, space? How do you relate to this part of who you are? And a lot of them think of it as very other; when they're thinking about who they are at their core, they don't seem to incorporate their different profiles. And then I thought I'd mention the selfies, since we're searching for the human face. And the selfie is, like, in an entire week we've got so many human faces everywhere. In fact, just before we started, I noticed two young women taking a selfie outside the bathroom and I remember thinking, What is it about this bathroom that requires a selfie? No offense if you're in the audience, but I did wonder that.

So, they were capturing a really wonderful moment, perhaps, in their friendship, and it just happened there. So, [*audience laughter*] anyway. This year, too, when you're walking around New York, have you seen the selfie sticks? Now we have even more ways to amplify our selfies. You know the stick where you put your phone at the end? I see people sometimes, I live down by the river in Brooklyn, and I have seen so many people—I can't tell you how many—with the stick out over the river, trying to take a picture, and I think, That's not a good idea. [*audience laughter*]

So anyway, I've asked all the students who've participated so far, What do you think of selfies? I might say about half of them will say right off the bat, "I hate selfies. Like, they're so ridiculous, people shouldn't take selfies." And then they'll say,"But I only take, like, seven or eight a day." [*audience laugher*]

Even students who sort of stand against selfies are participating in selfie culture, I guess you could call it. And a lot of them will roll their eyes about it, and the ones who do like it are very sheepish. They sort of know that they probably shouldn't, or they should be embarrassed about it, but then they'll gush about how much they love it. And you know, students will talk about how it's really hard to take a good selfie. Some of them spend a long time; they will take two pictures at a time in order to come up with just the one that they think is worth putting somewhere.

A lot of the students I spoke with have rules about selfies. They'll talk about how, like, "I don't selfie more than two to three times a week. You shouldn't do it every day, I hate those people who put up a selfie of themselves everyday. Like, I don't need to see you eating your hamburger." But then they'll be like, "I only do it twice a week," or "I only do it three times a week." So they've come up with structures for what is acceptable and what isn't, and they follow those rules. But a lot of them talk about how selfies are a lot of work, because getting them just right is complicated. And then they do 40 or 50 tries, or 35. I think heard 40 to 50 is sort of like an average. Like, you know, you take 40 to 50 pictures, and I'm like, You do?

You find the right one, and you try it out on a profile, whether it's on Instagram or Facebook. I can already tell you that Facebook is over. Facebook is just where you put your graduation pictures, and really it's all about Instagram. Facebook is for your grandparents, according to most of the students. So, they feel very obliged to post on Facebook. For the most part, they're currently enjoying Instagram and some other apps.

You put the picture up and then you wait and see if the public confirms that it is truly a good selfie. The way people learn that is by how many "likes" you get, and in the discussions about likes, and selfies, and how many you get, I learned about high traffic times. Does anybody know about high traffic times? The first time I heard about high traffic times, I thought, What? I can guess what that is, but tell me, and so students from all over the place will talk about how it's really important on a college campus that you post that face, your face, that beautiful picture you took, right around between the hours of four and five o'clock or about between seven and nine p.m., because that's when everybody's checking. Don't you post that selfie at seven a.m. because no one's on there and it's gonna get lost. And so students will strategically decide to post at four, so they can maximize their likes, and if they feel very dejected they often have a number they're going for—they want 30 likes, or 80 likes, or 120 likes. Some people have very high like aspirations. [*audience laughter*] And if they don't, if their new picture doesn't get that certain amount of likes, that's how they know to take it down and try again.

I want to move on to one of the most surprising things I learned about social media so far. At the end, I wasn't expecting at all when I did the study that so much emphasis is placed on the importance of appearing happy at all times. And so one of the things that's happened in our culture, particularly with young people, is they feel like it is very important to put on a happy face when you're online. To always post, only post positive things, never post anything negative, even something like, "Today I had a bad day." And where students are learning this is from their parents, from their teachers, too, because we have left the phase of social media where people are putting up those drunk pictures, or pictures of themseves smoking marijuana, or pictures doing all kinds of things that you're not supposed to do, even illegal things.

Because all of the young people that I spoke to had very much been educated into the notion that you are being watched at all times by people who will affect your future. And that means, you better watch it, but you have to make sure that you are doing the right thing online, that you are always saying the right thing, because your future employer may be looking at you. And, if you say something that offends that person, then that's it for you. Or if you do something, you know, if you take a picture that gets out there that is unflattering to you, then your whole future could be gone.

And so there is a sense of, "I must always be happy," and so students talked about the pressure to appear happy at all times, and there is a resentment about it, too, because they feel like nobody's being authentic online. Everyone is always just putting on this happy face, and I don't really buy it, but I've also gotta do it, too; and so this idea that we must aspire to a kind of perfection in our profiles is the big deal right now for college students. High stakes posting: because their profiles are very, very high stakes; everything is very high stakes for them.

And I wanted to mention, too, that most students, except in very specific circumstances, will tell you that you should never post about politics, and you should never post about religion, because those are the two things that most likely will offend your future employers. And they feel like one comment, one political remark, one religious remark could mean the difference between them getting a job and the other person who they're competing against who didn't say anything about their religion or politics, you know, with regard to their employers. So they're very, very careful. And I also want mention one student in particular who told me he was an aspiring politician. He talked on and on about how he needed to have a spotless online record, and he used that word again and again: *spotless*. So, I've gotta be spotless. He was first told that in 8th grade, when he was running for student body president. Eighth grade! And I thought, Well okay.

So now I want to mention the humanity of Snapchat. Many of you may know Snapchat, maybe you're on Snapchat. Others may not know what Snapchat is: Snapchat is this app, already kind of waning in popularity, but still pretty popular—I definitely saw the rise, like the burst of happening for Snapchat. And Snapchat is this app where, you know, you can take a picture of yourself, send a visual text, and then it disappears in ten seconds. That's the basic idea. Then of course people think of it as the sexting app, because it disappears in 10 seconds, the picture.

We've had a lot of newspaper articles about how people can take screenshots, so be careful. Students are all aware that you're playing with fire if you sext on Snapchat, they're all aware of the screenshot; but the reason I bring it up is because of what I mentioned before about the importance of appearing happy at all times. The humanity of Snapchat is that whatever you put on there disappears for the most part, unless in remote instances where someone is out to get you. In general, though, it disappears, and students love the disappearing act because they feel like it's one of the only spaces where they can just be silly and they can just be dorky and they can say, I'm having a bad day, make a frown and take a picture and send it to their friends, because then it disappears there's no evidence of it, at least in theory. And they are really longing for a space to be honest, to be who they really are.

And so students, when I would ask them about Facebook and Instagram—there's so much pressure with all the likes—but they all brightened up when I asked about Snapchat. They were, "Snapchat is so much fun." It's almost like their online playground, I would say. Which brings me to the fact that college students are craving anonymity online because of all this pressure to appear perfect with anything attached to their names. If it's attached to your name, you are responsible for it, maybe for the rest of your life.

There is no playing around with Facebook. People know that everyone's going to look at your Facebook page, so you better be careful. And so I think in many ways that the popularity of Snapchat comes from this longing to just be able to say whatever you want, or to just be goofy for awhile.

Along with Snapchat there are a number of other apps that have risen to huge popularity, one of which I literally saw the rise of: it didn't exist in the spring semester, but in September it did. It's called Yik Yak, and it basically pulls your GPS location so each college campus has a Yik Yak, and you have to be within a two-mile radius; basically, everybody on a college campus can be on the, you know, say like the Notre Dame Yik Yak, and it's anonymous. So it's a kind of an anonymous Twitter and it's whatever's going on in that campus. This is not to say that it's all nice and silly. A lot of the students, what they love about it is how mean everybody is and how honest they are. It's the place where you say the things that are really not politically correct. It's where you really, actually talk about what you believe, and how you feel, and then people up-vote it, and down-vote it, and then it disappears from the feed and then it's gone.

Or, you do things like...I remember a student who was like, Oh, you know, there are sometimes people, oh today, I'm just like sitting up in a tree and singing. Isn't that nice? So they just get to be goofy on that as well. One of the things that the popularity of these anonymous kinds of Twitter and/or the texting, the pictures that disappear, I think it really tells us something about the pressure that students feel about the public nature of online social media, of how impressive it can be; but then they innovate to find other ways to be themselves. I wanted to point that out.

I want to mention religion here. I asked all the students—like, any student who identified as particularly religious at the beginning of the interview—I asked them at some point, Do you ever post about your faith online, do you use social media as a forum for talking about your beliefs? And pretty much most students...for example, Catholics students would always be like, "No, no, it's not appropriate to talk about your religion in public," which I feel is very Catholic. [*audience laughter*]

But Evangelical students always talked about, "It's very important to post inspiring Bible verses." They felt very open to being open about their faith.

I wanted to mention two young people in particular I interviewed on this issue. I could go on and on about the religion thing, but that's another conversation. One young woman at an event at her college campus, when I asked her about her faith and social media, she said, "Well, God uses Facebook," and I said, "What? Like, does God have a profile? Like what does that mean?" And she said, "God uses Facebook to glorify God's self. You know, all social media is a tool for God's glory and God is working through us, to glorify God's self on social media." We had a long discussion about that, which was interesting.

Later on that same campus I had a young man who told me that Facebook, things like Facebook and Twitter, were false idols that people were so, so engaged in, that they interacted with it as if it was its own God, and that it got in the way of people's faith. He tried to distance himself from it on behalf of his faith.

I thought that I would close these particular remarks with just asking this question: What does social media mean in our search for the human face? A fundamental aspect of our humanity seems to be our inability to be perfect. To be human is to be imperfect, right? Yet young adults today find themselves living at least partially in a world where they are now being taught that they should appear perfect, that they should only appear happy—if they want a job, if they care at all about their futures—because online is forever, it's eternal. And every post you make is immortal, god-like; it lives on and on, even beyond you. And that's a pretty tall order to live with all the time.

SMITH: Great. Thank you, Donna. [*audience applause*] I'm a sociologist, and we sociologists specialize in generalizations, so I'm going to try to take a lot of specific particulars of observations and experience and try to generalize a little bit about some of the processes or causal mechanisms that may be going on with social media and human relationships and sense of self.

Just to sort of lay out on the table a number of arguments or possibilities that a lot of you will be familiar with, so that we can then sort of directly wrestle with them, or talk about them, refute them or whatever. I have about eight distinct possibilities, and I'm not going to elaborate on them very much at all. But the first is, What about social media might be concerning? What is it that does concern some people? Those that are more apocalyptic about it, what do they think is threatening? And so, I just want to name those things and then we can sort of think about them and talk about them.

The first thing I think that people are concerned about is that there's a thinning out, so to speak, of a kind of relationship, that there's a superficialization, so to speak, of relationships, that goes on with an overuse of social media. Meaning that the thin communities of social media friends may divert time and attention from the building of more direct, unmediated, face to face, and embodied relationships. People are worried that there's less of a sense of real people sitting down with each other, working out real relationships, that the distance is a problem somehow. And I should say I'm laying these things out not because I'm endorsing them and asking you to rally behind them or against them; I have mixed feelings about them. I'm just trying to lay them out as ideas.

This idea of a thinning of relationships reminds me of a quote from back in the 19th century. Karl Marx said that in modernity, "All that is solid melts into air." One wonders if there's something about social media that causes the solidity of face to face, real, concrete relationships to somehow melt into air.

There's a cartoon I use to try to convince my students to stop using social media during class. I try to appeal to their sense of humor. The cartoon is a man and a woman in bed with no clothes on, sitting next to each other, and it appears that they probably had just had sexual intercourse, except they're both on iPhones. The guy is saying, "That was the best text I've ever had."

So, you know, the sense of like, Wait a minute, why are you on your iPhone here? So that's the first idea. The second is, and this resonates a lot with what Donna said, there seems to be a concern that appearance and perceptions are distorting people's sense of what matters. I lived in North Carolina for a long time, and the North Carolina state motto was, "To be rather than to appear." The worry is that something in social media increasingly emphasizes appearance and perceptions. The public presentation of self, not the real selves that we are, and that somehow that would be distorting to human identity and experience.

A third mechanism or process that may be going on is the increased mediation of experience, and by this I mean that social media seem to create new layers of mediation, like layers of distance between the real phenomenological human experience and what's going on in the world and in human relationships. So much of reality already has become mediated to us through media images, where everything, or a very many things, come to us through images. And the digital revolution seems to accentuate and accelerate that, so that more and more of life is mediated, rather than directly experienced. Another concern is the corruption of civil, reasoned, public discourse.

In this kind of pluralistic, democratic society, people will have differences and need to be able to talk together about them, get along, and come up with policies and agreements that will seem to work. And the concern is that social media just invites people to be their worst selves, and invites them to be snarky, impersonal, and destructive in their exchanges online, and that this is not good for interpersonal relationships, clearly, but also for the common good, the health of civil society.

Another concern is that social media contribute to a kind of epistemic, individualistic subjectivism, and all I mean by that is, there's no authority out there I can really rely on; all I have is my sense of things, my personal subjective individual sense. This could come about, for example, by the fact that the Internet pretty much wipes out gatekeepers. You don't have Walter Cronkite telling you what's happening in the world; you don't have a book editor who tells you there's a book worth reading, don't read other books; you can search, everything's available, everything can dump into your lap, and then it's up to the individual to decide what they think, how they feel. This may actually be changing the way our brains think about who's reliable, what you can trust, and this puts the reliability of the authority back on each individual self, and all they have to go on is their own subjectivity.

Another concern has to do with a distraction with trivia, that when people take so many photos of their hamburger, or their kitten, or whatever, and just post, post, post, or the latest feeling or whatever happened this afternoon, this focusing of human attention on the immediate, most of which is trivial, rather than the long-term, weightier, consequential, big questions and relationships in life. Another concern that people have is the contracting of attention spans. Again, whether this is just grumpy old man conservative-types being grumpy or not, I know college professors who have been around a long time say, "Young people's brains have been formed in a way where they no longer know how to read, think through, and criticize a long and difficult text," which is what has traditionally happened in much of liberal arts education, because most texts that young people have to deal with in their lives are short, quick, they don't even have to use proper grammar in them.

And so it's not just a matter of what kind of relationships do I have, it's a matter of how am I learning what's an appropriate way to engage ideas.Do I have the kind of attention span that can work through long, difficult, complicated things? Again, if that's true—and I'm not necessarily endorsing it, but if that's true—it has real consequences for the nature of personal experience, the nature of engaging the world, and the nature of being part of a society. The world is extremely complicated and requires ongoing argumentation and working through problems. Another thing from an Abrahamic point of view, at least, and I would say human goods point of view, is there's a concern that social media are in some ways eliminating what traditionally might have been called *ˢabbath*, that is, you have a time in your life when things just get put down, or stop being paid attention to, or get turned off, or you just rest. The nature of social media seems to eliminate boundaries and schedules. Everything is available all the time, and the question is, again, What does that do to our sense of self in our experience in the world?

Finally, there is some concern that social media—and we'd have to think through how this works—but somehow that social media erode a commitment to social institutions, to real social institutions out in the world, to care about them, to invest in them, to build them, to uphold them and sustain them, that something about social media is radically privatizing, radically. I'll just choose what I want to do and exclude the things that I don't care about.

And so, I know people who really are very concerned that young people just are not invested in social institutions in a way that's necessary for a good society to carry on. Should we be troubled by a social media? Should we be worried that this is harmful? Again, I'm kind of ambivalent about it all. Having said that, now I want to bounce a question back to Donna that I thought of when she was speaking. I want to set up my question by relating something that I've heard reported by people in colleges who work with study abroad students, and that is: many college study abroad students come back from overseas reporting that when they got to their study abroad side that was offline, the first week they were completely miserable because they couldn't be checking everything all the time, and they didn't know how they were going to live; and after one week, the rest of the semester they had a wonderful time, felt completely liberated, and thought life was wonderful, that it was fantastic. But when their study abroad was over, then they had a depressing reentry time, a sort of like, Oh, now I need to get all back into this world of social media.

So with that in mind, and that seems to be telling us something, my question for you, Donna, is there seems to be a duel nature going on here between an attraction to, an interest in really getting something out of social media, and almost a dependence on it, but also an alienation from something that's oppressive about it, that we really wish it wasn't this way; and a feeling of powerlessness to do anything about it. Do you have any thoughts aboutthe paradox of feeling oppressed or alienated, but also attracted to and really enjoying this experience?

FREITAS: I have data on that. So much, in fact, that I haven't counted up everything. I'm just gonna give you general numbers. One of the things I did not know when I did my very, very first interviews, I didn't have a segment of questions on smartphones. And the first three interviews I did, every single one of those students, the first three that I interviewed, just brought up smartphones on their own and the role of smartphones in their life and how you socialize or don't. And I suddenly realized, Oh my god, how did I miss that whole category? I'm gonna have a whole category of questions just on their relationship to their smartphones. I had so many students who, unprompted, said something like, Oh my gosh, you know I went and I did Spring Break in India or something—I went to India and my smartphone didn't work there, I didn't have any service at all, and it was so amazing not to like, be on my phone all the time. And everybody I was with, they weren't on their phones either, and we talked to each other way more, and the friends I made on the trip are way better than the ones I had before. And I had this one young woman in particular—she was a total surfer girl, she was always swimming—and she told me, Oh my gosh, I was leaning over the seawall one day with my phone, and then I dropped it into the water, and I was like, Oh no! This is so horrible! She was so expressive, and she goes, So, I spent the whole day without my phone, and by the end of the day it was like I came up out of a fog, and everything was so clear, I almost didn't wanna get it fixed.

So many students had stories like that, of how strange and wonderful it was to live without their smartphones, to not be able to just access, access, access. That said, I asked him, Well, so have you thought about getting rid of your smartphone? You know, if life is so much better? Well no, because it's like an obligation to have one today, you know, because my parents need to reach me, people need to reach me. Students feel like it's an obligation to be reachable now, and they also feel it's a burden. I learned that I needed to ask the question: Do you ever feel like your smartphone is like a job? Because so many students talk about the burden of responding too often, like 300 texts a day, how they feel overwhelmed, but at the same time they also feel like you're not allowed to live anymore without the stuff.

Many of them talked about how, even if they didn't want to be on social media, they felt like it was really important to their future careers to have a profile because, you know, you're damned if you do and you're damned if you don't. If people search for you and they can't find anything, they think something's wrong with you; but then if they search you and find, you know, you drinking beer, then something's also wrong with you. You've got to be searchable, but when you are searchable, you've got to have a very particular profile.

I spend so much time talking to students about the different ways they try to curb their usage. They come up with all these tricks, and they have all kind of rituals. Like a lot of students, I had a number who said the way they dealt with this was to leave the house in the morning without their charger, and once the phone ran out they had to let it go.

I spent a lot of time thinking about this. Let's take the Catholic tradition. Don't wire your churches, okay? Students are looking for an oasis where they don't have wifi, because that helps them. I often think, Boy, do we make a mistake to have every nook and cranny of our campus wired. Because students don't feel like they have the willpower to resist; the only way they can is if they're, like, in India, and they don't have service.

So I do feel like we need to have an oasis where they can't access the Internet. Students at Catholic schools—sometimes they'll talk about going on retreats, and how they went on a wireless retreat, they had to set the cell phone aside. One of the things that I think is really useful about the Catholic tradition, for example, are these practices, or these rituals, or these spaces, that we have in our life where, you know, once a week or once a year, if you want to you can retreat to where we have to unplug. I hope you all can think about that: students are looking for ways to ritualize their unplugging, they're looking for help unplugging; maybe not always, but at least sometimes. Students talked about how hard it was, the ones who went to church, to not do Snapchat in church. I'm like, You're doing Snapchat in church? You're taking selfies of yourself in the middle of church?

But a lot of them say, My rule is I can't be online in church. And they really cherish, say, Mass, just the opportunity once a week to have an hour where they're not online, where they're expected not to be online, is really huge for them. I think we all need to really reckon with that. I'm sure this place is wired too; I haven't tried it.

SMITH: I always say, when I'm talking about my own research on youth, that I think it's really important. Even though both of us study youth, and a lot of the focus on social media focuses is on youth, I think it's very, very important for those of us who were older to acknowledge that this is not a standard, "Oh, the kids these days" kind of probem; this is embedded in the adult world, the adult capitalist society and institutions. The children are being raised a certain way, by certain kinds of people, with certain kinds of institutions that they're being socialized into. They're particularly adept at using it and doing creative things with it, but we really—it would be a huge mistake to fall into the "Oh, the kids these days," as if adults are not implicated, not fully dragged down into all this stuff.

This last summer I went to Mass in Brooklyn and a fifty-some year-old woman got a cell phone call in the middle of Mass and stood up and had the conversation right there. There were other people appalled, but my point is, it's not just kids. Whatever is going on with young people, I think, is a good barometer of what's going on in our larger culture in society. So just to bracket that, to keep it in mind.

FREITAS: Well, on the subject you mentioned on the thinning of relationships, I think everyone gets really worried that young adults are not going to know how to conduct relationships, they are not meeting each other face to face now because the thing is social media. What I found out was really the opposite, which shocked me. What I found out from college students was they all think adults are nuts, because they do online dating, and they think that's crazy, that they'll just meet someone online and then go have sex or whatever, meet their partner online, and that is just a world away for them.

In general, they all want to meet people face to face. People are always talking about online learning, and that's great, even online universities; but I can tell you that students cherish the fact that college, a residential college, or just being in classes with other people, is a way for them to meet face to face. They want to meet each other face to face, they want to meet their friends face to face, they want to meet them on their football team, in a cross country team, in the band, and whatever other activities that they do. And so the idea that they would develop relationships, that relationships would start online, is pretty horrifying to them, even if they may use social media as a tool in forwarding that relationship or in keeping in touch with someone. But in general they all feel like it is not, it cannot be the substance of my relationship. It can be a tool in it but it's not central.

SMITH: One question that I have for myself, and I'd be interested in hearing what you think, is why is there this immense, powerful compulsion or attraction to this close relationship with social media? And I could think of different things. I mean, one argument is simply that human beings are incredibly hyper-social animals. We're just incredibly social, so give us any ways to be social and, except for those introverts among us, we'll be incredibly social all the time. It's not displacing their face to face relationships, they're just adding on to it several other ways to be social. That's a pretty benign view of things.

Another possibility is that there's some deep profound insecurity in us as human beings, that we're just not okay with solitude and silence. That they're trying to fill that up, and this argument goes all the way back to the Walkman—you know, from the '80s or whatever, with earphones—but that we can't stand silence, that we have to escape something with noise and interaction and trivia. If that's true, that would be really good to know. And whichever of these ideas are true, they'll have implications. You were just talking about getting offline almost as a new spiritual discipline. That's something to think about. Again, from an Augustinian perspective, you could think, Well, maybe people are searching for God and looking for otherness, and in trying to find so many relationships, that there's some search for the good here that maybe misdirected or distorted or incomplete somehow.

I just sorta I think it behooves us to try to dig deeper; what itches do social media scratch for people of all ages? Because it's clearly a powerful thing that people are locked into and attached to, and the more we can understand what is that attachment, what part of the brain is lighting up so to speak, and why, and what does that reflect about our condition or our situation in the world? That's the kind of question I think we really need to be asking.

FREITAS: I think one of the things that surprised me most is how deeply the college students that I spoke with are thinking about social media and how it's affecting who they are, their relationships, etc. One of the things that really stunned me was, at the very end of every interview, I asked every single student, Is there anything we haven't talked about yet, with regard to social media, that's particularly fascinating to you, or interesting to you, that worries you, and I just left it open. And I had a number of students who said, You know, I really worry about our inability to be alone today.

We're never alone anymore. I had a bunch of students who talked about their inability to just be still, their inability to be alone, and I thought, Huh. And students—I'm sure you've heard this—they talk about how pulling out the smartphone is the new yawn, it's a way to sort of, like, cut the conversation or show you're not interested, and it's also the cover-up for all awkward moments. And so students talked a lot about how,they worry that we're not learning to get through those awkward moments, that we're leaning on our smartphones too much to sort of cover up our inability or our fears of communicating with each other. Our fears of looking our friends in the eyes when we're talking. I was really amazed by how deeply students are thinking about how it's affecting who they are, what they do, how to interact with others, their capacities, their struggles.

For those of you who are coming from religious communities today—I think probably most of you are—I would encourage you as communities to think about the ways in which you can not just use social media as a tool in your communities, but figure out ways to bracket social media in the community that you create, because I can tell you that you'll be doing a service, certainly to the young people in your community.We all struggle with these things, we all have that impulse to grab our phone, and I think probably many of us are thinking that maybe we're not so far away from the young people in our communities as we might imagine.

SMITH: Donna, I would love to have had a Q&A hour following up here, to really hear all your thoughts, because obviously you've been wrestling with this stuff and thinking about it, and no doubt have a lot of great questions and ideas. But the format of the program doesn't allow for that, so it's really our hope that by just laying out these ideas here that this session will have stimulated you're thinking, giving you more ideas to chew on, and that we will continue to carry on a conversation the rest of today, this weekend, as you go home, in your own minds, with the kids you work with, or have in your school. Thank you, carry on the conversation. Thank you very much.

CPSIA information can be obtained at www.ICGtesting.com
Printed in the USA
BVOW06s2023070116

432160BV00006B/11/P